RACINE

PHAEDRA

RACINE

PHAEDRA

An English Acting Version

INTRODUCTION AND TRANSLATION

BY BERNARD D. N. GREBANIER

BARRON'S EDUCATIONAL SERIES, INC.
GREAT NECK, NEW YORK

A translation of Racine's Phaedra
by Bernard D. N. Grebanier

© 1958 Barron's Educational Series, Inc.
Great Neck, N. Y.

Designed by Stefan Salter

PRINTED IN THE UNITED STATES OF AMERICA

To

ALTHEA URN,
poète exquise

A NOTE ABOUT THIS VERSION

I know from experience that, given suitable production, *Phaedra* cannot fail on the boards, although it has not been seen in New York for decades in a professional performance. I have twice directed my version, once with a highly gifted college group (during this run a producer was so much impressed that he later negotiated a purchase from me of an option for a presentation with Miss Judith Evelyn as star), and again with a semi-professional group. Though the audiences for these were quite different from each other, they were always held spellbound by Racine's tragic greatness.

English-reading people are used to some stage directions when they approach a printed play. The very long blocks of speeches as they appear in French, without a direction or an emotional cue, are bound to prove discouraging to our reading public (and our directors and actors too!). I have therefore retained a certain minimum of the stage directions and emotional cues which I worked out while I was directing the play. I have also indicated the very simple set we used, which proved extremely effective. I cannot see how these should do otherwise than aid the reader, for I have made explicit only what I found implied in Racine's lines. The extreme purist, in any event, has only to ignore them.

I have tried, of course, to be faithful to every word of the original. To be faithful to the whole, however, has required that my version should be acceptable as English verse in its own right. The rhymed couplet, so noble and elegant on the French stage in the hands of its masters, is in English stilled and artificial; I therefore thought it best to use the noblest medium of our own stage, blank verse. That was not the only problem: the abstractions which Racine knew how to point up with fire have a tendency in English to sound hollow and stale—in my judgment, the chief difference in the genius of the two languages. I have therefore deliberately chosen to be specific and concrete where the original is generalized and abstract. Except in this matter, however, I labored never to ignore or transfigure any turn of thought in the original. For these reasons, I think of this version as both a translation and an adaptation.

July 1, 1958   B. D. N. G.

PREFACE

Phaedra[1] is to the French-speaking world what *Hamlet* is to the English—the crowning glory of their stage. Just as the register of actors who have performed Shakespeare's masterpiece is the register of our greatest actors in every period, so the roll-call of actresses who have appeared in Racine's great tragedy is the record of the greatest actresses the French have had. This was the role associated most with Rachel and the Divine Sarah. Certainly no part in any play demands more of the leading performer.

Racine was pleased to acknowledge his indebtedness to Euripides for *Phaedra,* but he owes very little to his master. No other dramatist would have been capable of creating this play, unrivalled for its intensity of passion. Here every look, every movement of muscle or body has a meaning. From the moment of Phaedra's entrance the air is charged with smothered violence. We are ensnared in an illusion of reality so vivid, that we cannot deflect our attention for a heartbeat. Step by step the tension is tightened—if allowed to grow laxer for a few minutes, only that it may be drawn the tighter soon after. Time ceases to exist, and as we watch, awe-struck, the unwindings of this simple plot, we "see into the heart of things."

It is, indeed, the unrelieved intensity of this play which

---

[1] *Racine's original title was "Phèdre et Hippolyte"* (Phaedra and Hippolytus). *In 1687 ten years after its first presentation, the tragedy's title was changed to "Phèdre."*

is responsible for its being a stranger to the English-speaking stage.

If *Phèdre* has been to the French stage what *Hamlet* has been to the English, it is no less true that as a writer of tragedy Jean Racine (1639-1699) is to his country what Shakespeare is to the English-speaking world. Many would add that, like the Englishman, he is also his country's greatest poet.

The Neoclassical school, which was at its height during his lifetime, is to be seen in its perfect flowering in his works. Clarity, lucidity, and simplicity, the cardinal virtues propounded by that school, however favorable to the development of fine prose, would not seem necessarily auspicious to the inspiration demanded for the writing of great poetry or great tragedy. In England, for example, these virtues proved more of a blight in both fields. In Racine's work, however, we find a man whose exquisite delicacy of understanding and taste was utterly at home within what, to English poets, proved constricting confines. For his genius he had the wisdom to be born at the perfect time in the right country.

He was born at La Ferté Milon, near Soissons, on December 21, 1639—more than thirty years after his greatest predecessor in French tragedy, Corneille. His father was a controller of the salt office, an important governmental post, and his family was connected with the Jansenist movement.

The Jansenists, a religious order with headquarters at Port-Royal, had been subject for some while to persecution because of their extreme views on the doctrine of original sin. They were accused of very nearly adopting the

Protestant (and therefore in France heretical) doctrine of predestination. Racine's parents both being dead by the time he was four, Jean was raised by his Jansenist grandmother, and sent by her to the Jansenist college at Beauvais. From there he went to a Jansenist school near Port-Royal. Besides learning the austere religious precepts of his teachers, he developed a love of the Greek of Euripides. His studies were completed at the college of Harcourt. It was his family's hopes that he would enter the Church. At first he seemed destined to take orders; but by 1663 he had decided that poetry was his true vocation, and he came to Paris. An ode written to celebrate the King's recovery from illness brought him a substantial present from Louis XIV.

His first plays, *La Thébaïde* (1664)—on the rivalry between the two sons of Œdipus—and *Alexandre* (1665)—on Alexander the Great—were both produced by Molière's troupe. It was they who brought Racine his first public successes. Without reason Racine played Molière a very shabby trick: he gave *Alexandre* to the only rival company in Paris, so that the tragedy was produced at both theatres at the same time. Racine's ingratitude went further: he persuaded Molière's best actress to join the rival troupe. Molière was, understandably, very angry; thus terminated what might have proved a highly valuable friendship between the two greatest geniuses of the age.

Meanwhile, Racine's friends and relatives at Port-Royal were becoming much concerned for Jean's increasing worldliness: his writing for the theatre was, in their eyes, sheer ungodliness. Despite all he owed to them, he next attacked the Jansenists in a brilliant and witty public *Letter*. He was about to follow this up with a second assault on his old friends when Boileau, his mentor and great admirer, restrained him, pointing out to him that the Jansenists were already sufficiently persecuted.

It was with *Andromaque* (1667) that he came into his own as the first dramatist-poet of his age. For the next ten years he composed a series of tragic masterpieces which are the highest achievements of the French theatre: *Britannicus* (1669), *Bérénice* (1670), *Bajazet* (1672), *Mithridate* (1673), *Iphigénie en Aulide* (1674), and *Phèdre* (1677); he also wrote the delightful satire on the legal profession, *Les Plaideurs* (1668). In 1664 he was appointed to a post at Court, and in 1673 he became a member of the French Academy.

Until the appearance of *Andromaque* Corneille had been the leading French dramatist; with that play's success Racine became a challenger for that position. Popular though he was at Court, and sought after by everyone, he was sensitive to the point of morbidity to the least criticism, and often responded in prefaces which were astonishing for their bitterness. Sad though it is to report, Racine was a very vain man, jealous of the success of others, and capable of incredible ingratitude. To have known Racine personally was assuredly not to love him.

At last his enemies were able to rout him from the stage. A powerful noblewoman encouraged a second-rate writer to do a play on the same theme as Racine's *Phèdre,* bought up the tickets of both houses, and arranged that Racine's masterwork be attended only by a hissing clique.

Though this failure was brief and temporary, it served

to turn Racine from the theatre. He interpreted it as a
judgment from God for his base disloyalty towards his
Jansenist friends, and he returned to Port-Royal to make
his peace with them. He was, indeed, ready to enter a
cloister. His spiritual adviser, however, counseled him to
marry. He did so, and raised seven children. His last years
(from 1677 to 1699) were devoted to his family and to the
King as Royal Historiographer. As time went on, he became more and more devout and confirmed in his Jansenist
views.

His period of great creativeness ended, as has been seen,
in his late thirties. But that did not mean any diminution
in his powers. Suddenly in 1689, after a lapse of a dozen
years, he returned to dramatic composition at the request
of Mme de Maintenon, when he wrote *Esther* for her
pupils at St. Cyr. Two years later he wrote his last and
noblest work, *Athalie* (1681), which was performed at
Versailles before the King without scenery or costumes; the
public was not to see this tragedy until more than fifteen
years after Racine's death. When he died in 1699, Racine
was buried at the Port-Royal cemetery.

As has been said, in Racine we find Neoclassical tragedy
at its best. It has been humorously suggested that the three
unities of the Aristotelian commentators seem to have been
invented just for Racine's purposes. If this is true in spirit,
it is somewhat owing to the fact that he always reduces
plot to a minimum. Tragedy, with him, always centers
on a single moral crisis. There is always a sense of great
simplicity and artistic purity in his plays. He himself said,
in the preface to *Bérénice*: "Real invention consists in

making something out of nothing." True genius, he maintained, can maintain interest through five acts not by "a multitude of incidents" but by "a simple action, sustained by the passions, the beauty of the ideas and the elegance of the expression." It would be hard to state more precisely the source of Racine's own greatness.

Though he has depicted magnificently political ambition, court intrigue, religious exaltation, and maternal love, Racine is above all the dramatist of the passion of love between man and woman. That is his most recurrent theme. Curiously, despite Racine's elegance, his women of passion talk with the violence of life itself; their emotion reveals itself in naked truth. It is the absence of plot complications which underlines every shade of feeling experienced by the characters in his tragedies.

As a stylist he is no less astonishing for his precision than for his restraint. Such simplicity as his is the product of a superb artistry harmonizing the word with the meaning.

Voltaire observed that every page of Racine ought to be annotated with "Beautiful, sublime, wonderful."

Bernard D. N. Grebanier

Brooklyn College
July 1, 1958

RACINE

PHAEDRA

CHARACTERS

Pronunc. in ink from Webster's New World Dict.

[hē-sūs] ; [mē-ròss]; [thē-pēs]

THESEUS, son of Aegeus and King of Athens

[fēl-drā a]

PHAEDRA, wife of Theseus and daughter of Minos and
Pasiphaë *(sister to Ariadne)*

[hǐ vǐ ə]

HIPPOLYTUS, son of Theseus and Antiope, Queen of the
Amazons

ARICIA, princess of the royal blood of Athens

ē nō nī (one source gives ee—shown noun)

OENONE, Phaedra's nurse and confidant

THERAMENES, tutor to Hippolytus

ISMENE, Aricia's confidant

PANOPE, Phaedra's waiting-woman

GUARDS

The scene is laid at Troezen, a town of the Peloponnesus

*Trēē-zayń (pron. from Appleton-C.
ppr. ed of Phèdre.*

Ēe-mōon " "

Icarus — ik' ə rəs, Ī kə rəs

ACT ONE

A couch, facing diagonally from downstage; a classic chair also diagonally situated—both with rich stuffs gracefully draped over. Three steps in the back lead to a heavily curtained entrance between tall columns. There are also a few low steps leading off upstage. Simple heavy drapes from either side the columns complete the set. There are five entrances.

[*Enter* HIPPOLYTUS *and* THERAMENES]

HIPPOLYTUS: My plan is fixed.

[*Walks down the steps,* THERAMENES *following*]

                    I leave, dear Theramenes,
to quit the precincts of fair Troezen's shores,
for I begin to blush at being idle.
A deadly doubt disrupts my peace of mind;
for six months separated from my father,
I own no knowledge of his precious life—
nor even know what lands can hide him now.

    THERAMENES: And in what lands, my lord,
                      mean you to seek him?
Already, to content your troubled breast,
I have traversed two seas[2] on either side
of Corinth,

[*Turning away, he recreates the distances he traveled*]

            sought for Theseus midst the peoples
on shores where Acheron[3] is lost among

---

[2] the Ionian and the Aegean.

[3] river in Hades.

3

the dead—and Elis[4] visited, and passed
by Taenarus[5] into the waters[6] where
winged Icarus [7] in hapless flight from Crete
once fell. And now,

    [*Turning to* HIPPOLYTUS]

                    on what new hopes,
in what mild clime, do you propose to find
his footsteps' trace? Indeed, how is it certain
your royal father wishes that we know
the secret of his absence?

    [*Ironically*]

                        While we fear
his fate, that hero may be calmly waiting,
keeps guarded from our ears his newest loves,[8]
until some poor deluded woman has—

HIPPOLYTUS: [*Hotly*]
Cease, Theramenes, cease! He is your King!
His youthful follies tempt him now no more;
no such dishonoring impediment
detains him. His inconstancy to Phaedra
he's ended, swearing solemn oaths: it's long
since she's had cause to fear a rival love.

---

[4] *on the west coast of the Peloponnesus.*

[5] *in southwest Laconia.*

[6] *the Aegean Sea.*

[7] *the son of Daedalus, the inventor. When they were escaping from Crete, each wearing wings made by Daedalus, Icarus flew too near the sun. The heat melted his wings' fastenings of wax, and he fell to death in the sea.*

[8] *Theseus had a long career of winning the love of women and then abandoning them.*

To seek him now is but my filial duty—
   [*Impetuously*]
I fly a land I hope no more to see!
   THERAMENES: Indeed? You *dread,* my lord,
                         the look of this
most tranquil site, so rich in memories
of childhood, where I've seen you choose to be
when Athens' court and all its stately bustle
invited you? What jeopardy, what grief
(I rather say) can drive you from your home?
   HIPPOLYTUS: The happy time you speak of is no more.
   [*Passionately*]
A change has come on everything since Heaven
saw fit to send Queen Phaedra[9] to our shores.
   THERAMENES: I understand. I know your cause of grief:
it's Phaedra who disturbs you, who offends
your sight. A threatening stepmother, she scarce
had looked upon you when she proved her power
at once and banished you from Athens. Yet ponder:
her hate, first fleshed on you, is now assuaged—
relaxed, at least. Besides, what danger could
pursue you from a dying woman longing
for death? Made prostrate by a disease which she
refuses to have ministered, can Phaedra,
self-weary, tired of the light of day,
form any plots against your present peace?
   HIPPOLYTUS: It's not *her* futile enmity I fear.
Another enemy persuades my flight.
I fly, the truth is, from Aricia,

---

[9] *Racine here refers to her as "the daughter of Minos and Pasiphaë."*

the last survivor of a race[10] that's doomed
to plot against our line.

    THERAMENES: My lord, then you
must persecute her too? That lovely princess
has never steeped herself in intrigues framed
by her perfidious brothers! And why should you
detest her innocent allurements thus?

    HIPPOLYTUS: [*dejectedly*]
Ah, were it hate I feel, I should not fly.

    THERAMENES: [*Placing a fatherly hand
on* HIPPOLYTUS's *shoulder*]
My lord, will you not tell me why you fly?
    [*Humorously*]
Are you indeed that proud Hippolytus,
the foe implacable of love's decrees—
those bonds to which your father has so oft
submitted? Is it Venus, long misprized
by your self-pride, who now will justify
at last your father? Has the goddess ranged
you with the rest of mortals? Does she force
your worship at her shrines? Can you too love?[11]

    HIPPOLYTUS: My friend, what are you saying?
                       You've known my heart
since first it beat; do you require I
humiliate myself and disavow

---

[10] *The fifty sons of Pallas, cousins of Theseus, conspired against
him when he first came to the throne, to gain the crown of
Athens, which they asserted was theirs by right. Theseus slew
them all.*

[11] *Hippolytus has thus far disdained love.*

my heart's professed disdain? With that same milk
my Amazonian mother[12] gave me suck
she fed the pride you wonder at. When ripe
in years, I only could approve that learning.
Then, bound in love to me, your charge, you told me
the story of my father. Well you know
how oft my soul, attentive to your voice,
was animated by the tale of his
renowned exploits when you depicted me
the noble hero who atoned to men
their loss of Hercules, the monsters quelled,
the robbers punished—Cercyon, who killed
all strangers whom he overcame in wrestling—
and Sciro, causing all his captives lave
his feet as on his cliff he sat, and whence
he kicked them in the sea—Procrustes, who
enforced his bed of torture on the luckless
who innocent besought a sheltered night—
and mighty Sinnis, who from tops of pines
the scattered bodies of the men he seized
would catapult into the air—the bones
dispersed of Epidaurus' giant, whose club
the traveler had come to hold in dread—
the Minotaur, half man, half bull, with blood
of whom Crete's city reeked, the offspring foul
of this Queen Phaedra's mother.[13] When you told

12 *Antiope.*
13 *For the purposes of stage production I have taken the liberty of
briefly expanding this passage. The original merely says: "the
robbers punished—Procrustes, Cercyon, and Sciro, and Sinnis,*

these shining deeds my father wrought to cleanse
the earth, my bosom glowed with pride.

   [*Walks away disconsolately*]

                            But when
you told me of his acts less glorious,
his solemn oaths broadcast and credited
by hundreds—Helen stolen from her kin
in Sparta[14]—Salamis the witness of
the tears of Periboea[15]—so many others
whose very names escape me—credulous
poor souls betrayed by Theseus' passion: sad
abandoned Ariadne[16] murmuring
his faithlessness to senseless rocks, and last,
with kinder issue, Phaedra carried off.
You know with what regret I heard those tales,
and pressed you oft to stop the story, glad
if I could kill the memory of that part
unworthy of so excellent a life!

   [*With anguish*]

And I, in turn, am I to feel this yoke?
And will the Gods behold me thus debased—
my sluggish sighs the more despicable

---

*and the bones dispersed of Epidaurus' giant, and Crete reeking
with the blood of the Minotaur." This is the only place where I
found it expedient to add to the text.—B.D.N.G.*

[14] *before her marriage to Menelaus. She was still a child.*

[15] *Racine is slightly in error here. It was after Theseus abandoned
her that Periboea married Telamon, King of Salamis.*

[16] *who made it possible for him to kill her half-brother, the Minotaur. He eloped with her and Phaedra, her sister. Ariadne he
abandoned at Naxos.*

that such a hoard of honors must excuse
my father? For no monster overcome
by *me* gives me the right to err like him.
And even if my spirit must be softened,
need I have made Aricia my tamer?
Can my defrauded senses have forgot
the barriers eternal which divorce us?
My father disapproves; his laws severe
forbid that line increase; he fears the shoot
from out a stock so culpable; with her
he wishes to entomb their very name.

[*Shaking his head*]

She must submit to him, her guardian:
she'll never see her torch of marriage lit!
Am I to champion her rights against
an angry father—stand the world's example
for rashness? Shall my youth embark upon
a sea of folly—?

THERAMENES:

          Ah, my lord, when once
the hour's appointed, God takes little note
of all our logic.

[*Moves off*]

          Theseus, hoping but
to seal your eyes, has opened them. His hate,
which feeds your rebel flame, but lends new grace
to her, his foe. And why, indeed, should love
that's chaste affright you? Love is sweet, and dare
you taste none of its sweetness? Must you nurse
these morbid scruples? Do you fear to walk

the path which Hercules could pace? What heart
so brave but Venus knew to vanquish it?
Yourself, who spite the goddess, where were you
if great Antiope[17] had likewise scorned
her laws, and never burned with modest heat
for Theseus? Why affect so proud a speech?
Admit love, all must change. For many days
I see you less and less in wonted sport;
disdainful of the world you were and proud,
now racing your swift chariot along
the shore, now, skilled in Neptune's science[18] as
the god himself, the untamed courser making
submissive to the bit. Less frequent do
the woods reverberate our shouts.

   [*Pointing an accusing finger, in amusement
at* HIPPOLYTUS]

                              Some secret
has dulled your eyes. How can I hold a doubt?
You are in love—you are consumed with love!

   [*With humor*]

You languish in this sickness you conceal!
Are you not smitten by Aricia?

   HIPPOLYTUS: [*Avoids his glance, and then suddenly
starts to move off*]

I go to find my father, Theramenes.

   THERAMENES: My lord, you will not take
                              your leave of Phaedra?

_____

[17] *Hippolytus's mother.*
[18] *making the untamed steed "submissive to the bit."*

HIPPOLYTUS: [*Pausing*]

I don't intend to see her. You can tell her.

[THERAMENES *shakes his head, disapprovingly*;
HIPPOLYTUS *is shamed into staying*]

Well then, I'll see her since it is my duty.

[*Looking off*]

But what new sorrow vexes her Oenone?

[*Enter* OENONE]   *Act I, Scene 2*

OENONE: Alas, my lord, what sorrow equals mine?
The Queen now feels her mortal end approaching.
In vain I keep through day and night my watch
by her. She's dying of an illness she
conceals from me. Her spirit is the prey
of a remorseless perturbation. Her
unceasing fretfulness exiles her sleep.
She yearns to see the sun, but her profound
disquietude excludes all visitors. . . .

[*Looking off*]

HIPPOLYTUS: Enough,

OENONE: She comes.

[*Goes off to help* PHAEDRA]

HIPPOLYTUS: I leave her here. I'll not
disturb her with the sight of one she loathes.

[*Exeunt* HIPPOLYTUS *and* THERAMENES, *as* PHAEDRA
enters on OENONE's *arm*]   *Act I Scene III (Ph's confession to the nurse)*

PHAEDRA: [*Staggering to couch, on which she leans
heavily*]   *Imitated from Euripides*

Let's go no further. Stay, Oenone, dear.
I can no more bear up. My strength deserts me.

[*She sinks into the couch with exhaustion*]

*One of the 2 great scenes in play; other is
Ph's. avowal of love to Hipp – Act II, Sc 5
Imitated from Seneca*

My eyes are blinded by the light of day
I see again. My trembling knees give way.
Alas!

   OENONE: [*Moving around the back of the couch*]
     Almighty Gods! If but our tears
could still your wrath!

   PHAEDRA: How all these foolish jewels—
how all these veils weigh down on me!

   [*Tearing them off*]

                        Whose meddling
officious hand caught up my hair this way
and twined it in this pressing fillet? All
things crush me, all things wound me! Why must you
conspire to injure me?

   OENONE: [*Pleading*]
               Your every wish
is contradictory! Yourself but now
were blaming your unreasoned plans, and spurred
our hands to deck you out. Yourself, because
you felt again your former strength, did wish
to sally forth and see the sun again!
And now you see it, madam, would you hide
in hatred of the daylight that you sought?

   PHAEDRA: [*Not listening*]
Noble, radiant author of a race
that's doomed, O you my mother boasted as
her father![19] You who may well blush to see
me in my present sorrow! You, O Sun!

---

[19] *Phaedra's mother, Pasiphaë, was a daughter of the Sun.*

If this were but the last time I beheld you!

   OENONE: [*Annoyed*]

Again! Will you not cast aside this mad
intent? Must I forever hear you're sick
of living, and preparing in this style
lugubrious for death?

   PHAEDRA: [*Breathlessly*]

                You Gods! If I
might feel the cooling shade of forests!

   [*As in a trance*]

                       When
shall I with pleasured eye athwart the noble
race-ground-dust behold the chariot
in flight along the course again?

   OENONE: What say you?

   PHAEDRA: [*Startled at what she has revealed*]

Mad that I am, where do my senses lead me?
What do I say? Where do I let my soul
and my desires stray? I've lost my mind!
The Gods have reft me of my reason! Oh,
Oenone, shame makes red my face! You've seen
too clearly my disgraceful torture-rack!
My eyes, despite me, fill with guilty tears.

   OENONE: [*Not understanding*]

If you must blush, then blush that you won't speak—
your silence but excites the violence
of what you suffer. Obstinate against
our love for you, and deaf to all our words,
are you indeed so pitiless to end
your life? What rage must cut you off ere half

your days are done? What spell, what poison dries
the fountain of your life?

[*She moves behind the couch*]

Three times night's shadows
have hid the sky since sleep has closed your eyes;
three times the day has chased night's darkness since
your weary body languishes unnourished.

[*She moves behind* PHAEDRA *and hangs over her*]
What frightful plan do you allow to tempt you?
What right have you to dare this cruel attempt
against your very life? You do offend
the Gods, the authors of your being! You
betray both husband and the faith that binds you—
betray, indeed, your wretched children—

[*Shaking an admonitory finger at her*]

for you
will drag them down beneath a heavy yoke!
Remember that the day which robs them of
their mother is the day which gives new hope
to the barbarian's son, the enemy
implacable to you and to your line,
that son an Amazon has carried in
her womb, Hippolytus—!

PHAEDRA: [*Recoiling at the name*]
Oh Gods!

OENONE: [*Misinterpreting*]
Ah! This
reproach you feel!

PHAEDRA: You wretched woman, cease!
What name breathes forth your lips?

OENONE: [*With satisfaction*]

Alas, your wrath
is just enough. I like to see you quiver
when I pronounce that hated name. Then live!
    [*Lifting her arms in enthusiasm*]
Let love, let duty be the spurs to life!
Then live, and suffer not the Scythian's[20] son
to crush your children with his hated sway,
and give commands to yours, the richest blood
in Greece, descended from the Gods. Defer
no longer! Every moment is your slayer.
Restore at once your shattered strength while still
the nigh-extinguished flame of life is lit
and can be yet replenished to new light!

    PHAEDRA: [*Shuddering*]
Too long I have prolonged my sinful hours!

    OENONE: *What* sinful hours? By what remorse should *you*
be rent? What crime could weigh on you with woe
so heavy? When have hands of *yours* been steeped
in blood of innocents?

    PHAEDRA: [*Sickly*]

Thank the Gods,
my hands have never neared a crime! Oh would
to Heaven my heart were innocent as they!

    OENONE: What dreadful scheme, then, have you nursed,
                                        that strikes
your heart with terror?

    PHAEDRA: [*Bowing her head*]
                I have said enough.

---

[20] *Antiope's.*

I would be spared the rest. I die to spare
myself the bane of that indign confession.

   OENONE: [*Folding her arms across her chest,
in exasperation*]
Then *die,* and keep your stony-hearted silence!
But find some other hands to close your eyes!
Although you own at most the feeblest spark
of life, my soul shall find its death before yours.
A thousand open roads can lead me there.
My suffering will choose the shortest way.
Ah cruel! When has my loyalty betrayed you?
Forget you how when you were born it was
these arms that held you? Fatherland and children—
for you I gave up everything! Is this
the thanks I reap from you for my devotion?

   PHAEDRA: [*Wearily*]
What can this tempest bear but bitter fruit?
If I broke silence you would freeze with horror.

   OENONE: What horror can you tell, great Gods!,

                                  that's more

than seeing you expire before my eyes?

   PHAEDRA: When you shall learn my sin—

                              this curse that bows

me down—
   [*On the verge of tears*]
            I yet must die of it as surely!
I yet must die, and die the guiltier!
   [OENONE *hurls herself on her knees before her*]
   OENONE: By all the tears I've shed for you, my lady,
by your weak knees which I embrace with love,

release my spirit from this killing doubt!

[*She lays her head in* PHAEDRA's *lap and sobs*]

PHAEDRA: [*In a dead voice*]

It is your wish. Get up, then.

OENONE: [*Rising*]

        Speak, I hear.

PHAEDRA: Oh Heavens! What am I to say to her?
And how begin?

OENONE: Offend me now no more
with these vain terrors.

PHAEDRA: [*As in a trance*]

        Animosity
of Venus! Fatal hatred! Through what sore
distractions of wild love did you not hurl
my mother![21]

OENONE: [*Extending her hand in protest*]

    Lady, let them be forgot!
Let us forever hide that memory
in unbroken silence.

PHAEDRA: [*As before*]

       Ariadne, sister,
by what love wounded did you die on shores
far off, a stranger and forsaken![22]

OENONE: Ah,
Lady, why speak you so? What mortal pain
inspires you against your kinsfolk thus?

---

[21] *Her mother, Pasiphaë, had conceived a mad passion for a white
bull. The fruit of the monstrous union was the Minotaur.*
[22] *forsaken by Theseus, with whom she had eloped.*

*also called
Aphrodite*

PHAEDRA: Since Venus wills it, I shall die the last
of this unhappy and most tortured line!

OENONE: [*Recoiling*]

Are you in love?

PHAEDRA: I feel all passion's fury!

OENONE: For whom?

PHAEDRA: Now hear the top of earthly horrors!
I love—I tremble at that fatal name—
I shudder at its sound—I love—

[*She cannot continue*]

OENONE: [*Shrieking her impatience*]

                        Whom love you?

PHAEDRA: [*With desperate calm*]
You know the son of that great Amazon,
the prince so long oppressed by me!

OENONE: Great Gods!
Hippolytus?

PHAEDRA: [*In self-defense*]
            It's you have named him.

OENONE: [*Horrified*]

                                    Him!
The blood within my veins has turned to ice!
What criminality! Despair! O race
ill-starred! O journey fated ill! O land
accursed, did we have need to reach these shores
pernicious to our peace?

PHAEDRA: [*Lost in happy recollection*]
                        My malady
is ancient, older far than that. Yes, scarce
had I to Theseus bound myself in ties

of marriage, scarce my happiness seemed sure,
when Athens forced my foe upon my sight.
I saw him, blushed, and paled before his glance,
and trouble rose within my wildered soul.
My eyes could see no more, I could not speak.
I felt by turns my body chill and burn.
I recognized then Venus and her fires
unquenchable—relentless goddess who
pursues with torment unavoidable
my race! With fervent vows I thought to turn
aside her tortures—built a temple to her,
and lavished every ornament upon it.
Amidst my many offerings, myself
sought hourly my wandering reason in
their entrails. Powerless were they to cure
a love incurable!

   [OENONE *moves to columns and leans in sorrow against
one of them*]
                In vain my hand
burned incense on the altars. While my lips
called on the goddess' name, my heart adored
Hippolytus. Unceasingly I saw him—
yes, even at the altar's foot when it
was smoking! *He* was the god I dared not name—
his were the offerings! I shunned him when
I could. O depth of misery! My eyes
but traced him in his father's features. Then,
at last I stirred revolt against myself;
I pricked my courage, played the persecutor.
To banish him, the enemy I loved,

I took upon myself the pettishness
attributable to a harsh step-mother.
I urged his exile, and my endless cries
divorced him from his father's loving breast.

[*Peacefully*]

Oenone, then I breathed at last. When he
was gone my days ran smoothly once again
in innocence, submissive to my mate.
Unrest was silenced, and I attended to
the fruits of our ill-omened marriage.

[*With sudden anguish*]

                                                    Vain!

Precaution futile! Cruel destiny!
My husband brought me here himself, and here
I saw again the enemy I'd sent
away. Too soon my old wound bled anew!
No longer is it fire hidden in
my inmost heart.

[*She rises and staggers, in a frenzy*]

                        It's *Venus* who entire
has seized me for her prey![23]

[*With exhaustion*]

                                        I have conceived
full horror of this sin of mine!

[*She collapses weakly, and moves towards the couch*]

                                        I hold
my life in hate, my love itself in loathing!
I wished to keep my name unsullied through

---

[23] C'est Vénus toute entière à sa proie attachée.—*One of the most
celebrated lines in world drama.*

swift death—to hide from day so black a passion!
Withstanding tears and plaints of yours proved more
than I was able to contrive. I've told
you all, nor shall repent, provided that
you will respect approaching death and vex
me not with your unjust reproaches, and
will cease your vain attempt to fan to life
the flickering flame now anxious to expire.

[*She leans upon the couch. Enter* PANOPE]   *I: 4*

Scene 4

PANOPE: I would I might withhold sad news from you,
my lady, but I needs must tell the truth.

[*Weightily*]

Death has bereaved you of your dauntless husband.
These bitter tidings all know now but you.

OENONE: What say you, Panope?

[PHAEDRA *is stunned*]

                            The Queen would vainly
require of Heaven her noble lord's return.
By vessels now in port Hippolytus
has learned his father Theseus' *certain death.*

PHAEDRA: [*Overwhelmed at the alteration of
circumstances*]

Great Gods!

PANOPE: Now Athens is divided in
the choice of ruler. Some would give their vote
for the Prince, your son, my lady, while yet others
forgo the laws and cry allegiance to
the stranger's son, Hippolytus. They say,
indeed, one faction insolent would yield
the throne unto Aricia, the stock

of Pallas. Fit it is I warn you of
this danger, for Hippolytus already
prepares to leave. It's feared, if he appear
midst this disorder now, he'll draw with him
the fickle populace entirely.

OENONE: Enough, good Panope. The Queen, who
                                           hears you,
will not neglect your timely admonition.

[OENONE *motions her to go. She bows and goes out.*
OENONE *walks towards the chair in meditation*]

My lady, I no longer urged you live,
my thoughts already fixed on following
my mistress to the grave; no longer had
I strength to change your resolution. But
this new unhappiness prescribes now other
behavior. Fortune alters face; your lot
is *different.*

[*Stressing her words to wake* PHAEDRA'S *attention*]
            The King is *dead,* my lady:
his place devolves on *you.* His death leaves you
a son to whom you owe your duty—slave
if he should lose you—king if you will live.
To whom is he to look for help in his
bereavement, whom to dry his tears—but you?
His sobs of innocence the Gods will hear,
and they will move his ancestors to wrath
against his mother. Live! You've nothing to
reproach yourself! Your love involves no blame!
Your Lord in dying frees you from the bonds
which made the sin, the terror of your passion.

Hippolytus becomes no source of dread,
and you may see him now without a sense
of shame. His leading the sedition may
indeed proceed from his conviction of
your hate for him. As king of these most graced
and happy shores, *his* portion lies in Troezen.
He knows, however, that the laws bestow
proud Athens' ramparts now perforce upon
your son. Hippolytus and you possess
a foe in common: both unite and combat—
is my advice—this foe, Aricia.

    PHAEDRA: [*Almost against hope*]
Well then! I'll let your counsel carry me
along. If I can be restored to life,
I'll try to live. Perhaps a mother's love
in this funereal hour can animate
once more my enervated soul to life.

    [*Exeunt,* OENONE *leading* PHAEDRA]

ACT TWO

Scene 1

[*Enter* ARICIA *and* ISMENE]

ARICIA: Hippolytus has asked to see me here?
Hippolytus has sought me out to say
farewell? Ismene, is that true? You're certain?

ISMENE: It's but the first effects of Theseus' death.
Expect, my lady, now on every side
to see the hearts withheld from you by Theseus
revert to you. Aricia at last
is mistress of her fate, and soon all Greece
she will behold fall at her feet.

ARICIA: Ismene,
it's not some ill-established rumor, you
are sure? Am I indeed to be a slave
no longer?—have no enemies henceforth?

ISMENE: No, my lady. The Gods no more towards you
will prove unfriendly now that Theseus has
gone off to overtake your brothers' shades.

ARICIA: [*Sitting on couch*]
What mishap put an end to Theseus' days?

ISMENE: The rumors sown about his death are past
belief. They say he ravished a new maiden,
and that the waves engulfed that faithless husband.
They say as well (and this report is wide)
that he descended with Pirithoüs[24]

---

[24] *who assisted his good friend Theseus in abducting the child
Helen. Later, in exchange of favors, Theseus agreed to aid his*

24

into the world of shades—that Cocytus[25]
he's visited, and seen its sombre shores—
that he appeared alive among the ghosts
infernal, but knew not the path to leave
that melancholy sojourn, nor to trace
his steps back from those shores from which no steps
can ever hope retrace their way.

ARICIA: Shall I
believe a mortal, ere his final hour,
can penetrate the deep abode where dwell
the dead? What spell could draw him to those dreaded
banks?

ISMENE: [*Looks at her incredulously*]
        Theseus, sure, is *dead*, my lady!
and you alone must doubt it! Athens grieves,
and Troezen is apprized. The land already
acclaims Hippolytus as King.

[*With subtle rejoicing*]
                                And Phaedra,
who trembles in this very palace for
her son, seeks counsel from her troubled friends.

ARICIA: [*Rising and slowly moving*]
And you believe Hippolytus will prove
more kindly than his father? Will he loose
my chains? Or will he pity my misfortune?

---

friend in a bolder exploit: the abduction of Persephone from
Hades. The attempt failed and both heroes were kept prisoner
by the King of the Underworld. At length Theseus was freed by
Herakles; but his friend had to remain in Hades. It is of this
story that Racine is thinking.

[25] *a river in Hades.*

ISMENE: My lady, I indeed am sure he will.

ARICIA: You know not Theseus' callous son, I fear!
On what unfounded hope do you expect
he'll pity me, or single me alone
from out a sex he holds in scorn?

[*In a proud voice*]

You see
how long it is he has avoided me,
and seeks to be but where I am not found.

ISMENE: I know well every tale they tell of his
indifference. But I have seen this proud
Hippolytus when close to you, and when
I saw him, watched with doubled interest
the workings of his rumored haughtiness.

[*She shakes her head*]

His bearing no way answered to report:

[*Gently satirical*]

Your first glance troubled him; his eyes in vain
avoided yours, and, filled with languor, could
not leave your visage. Name of lover may
perhaps offend his pride; his *eyes* betray
he feels, no matter what his tongue denies.

ARICIA: Too eagerly, Ismene dear, my heart
hears hungrily your words, which may be based
on slender substance. You who know me well—
is it conceivable the plaything sad
of a relentless fate, a heart whose food
has been but bitterness and tears, might know
the balm of love and its mad sorrowings?

[*Sadly*]

Last offspring of a king, the noble son[26]
of Earth, I only have survived war's furies.
I've lost six brothers in their manhood's flower,

[*Very much the princess*]

their death the death of an illustrious line!
The sword has cut them down; the sodden soil
regretfully drank blood poured from the veins
of King Erechtheus' house. You know the law
severe which since their death forbids the Greeks
that any sue for my affection, for

[*With a touch of bitterness*]

it's feared a reckless flame for me might wake
to life the sparks yet flickering amidst
the ashes of my brothers. And you know
as well with what disdainful eye I've looked
upon such measures of that conqueror
suspicious.[27]

[*More gently*]

        How I have opposed my thoughts
to love, you also know, and how I've thanked
King Theseus oft for his injustice, whose
intended harshness happily assisted
my own aloofness.

[*Looking away, recollectively*]

        Eyes of mine that time—
my eyes had never yet beheld his son.
Not that my eyes alone, in timid shame

---

[26] *Erechtheus, from whom Aricia was directly descended.*
[27] *Theseus. See note 10 in Act I.*

enchanted, as they were, to note his grace
and beauty—all admire them—could cause
me love him merely for the gifts which Nature
endowed him with, and which he scorns himself,
or else knows nothing of!

[*Lyrically*]

                I love in him
and prize far nobler riches, qualities
his father gave unsullied by his faults.
I love, I vow, that noble pride itself
which will not bend beneath the yoke of love.
How vain for Phaedra that she glory in
the sighs of Theseus!

[*Joyfully*]

                I, more proud, disdain
to wear the shallow triumph when a thousand
fond women also share it, or to seek
a room within a heart that's ever open.

[*Triumphantly*]

To bow a heart that never yet has yielded,
to wake love's sorrow in a soul that never
has felt love's pains, to bind a captive who's
astounded at his fetters—who rebels
to no avail against the pleasing chains—
that is the triumph I desire, *that*
could stir me! To disarm great Hercules
were easier than young Hippolytus,
for *he* was vanquished often, overcome
too readily, and brought thus less of glory
to charms which conquered him.—

[*She runs to* ISMENE, *clasping her about the waist and hiding her head on her shoulder*]

Ismene dear,
how heedless I've become! Alas, I'm sure
indifference alone can meet my hopes!
Perhaps you'll hear me humbled with distress
bemoaning that same pride I now adore.
You think Hippolytus *can* love? What joy
sublime am I to feel that might make bend—?

ISMENE: [*Looking off, with humor*]
You'll hear him now speak for himself. He's coming.

[*Enter* HIPPOLYTUS. ISMENE *quietly retires*]

HIPPOLYTUS: Before departing, lady, I believe
I ought apprize you of your altered future.
My father is no more. My well-established
misgivings on his long-protracted absence
forbode the cause. Death, death alone could mark
the limits to his shining deeds, and hide
him from the knowledge of the world thus long.
The Gods at last deliver to the doom
of death the friend, companion, and successor
of Hercules. I think your hate, still just
unto his qualities, can hear these titles
without resentment. Hope—one hope alone
alleviates my mortal sorrow. I
can liberate you now from your severe
wardship, and I revoke the laws whose rigor
I have deplored. Pray, deem yourself as free
to order your affairs—and your affections—
as pleases you. In Troezen, which today

becomes my heritage, my grandsire's kingdom
of yore, and which with confidence acclaims
me as its king, I leave you free as I
myself—

[*Meaningfully*]
              yes, *freer.*

ARICIA: Moderate this kindness:
I am embarrassed by the excess of
your goodness. Honoring my plight with thoughts
so generous, my lord, you place me more
than you may guess beneath those rigorous
decrees from which you would release my lot.

[*He looks at her with gratitude before speaking; then,
with happy confusion:*]

HIPPOLYTUS: Unsure of whom to name as next in line,
first Athens speaks of you, then me, and then
of Phaedra's son.

ARICIA: Of me, my lord?

HIPPOLYTUS: I know—
I don't deceive myself—the ruthless law
excludes *my* claims, for Greece reproaches me
because my mother's foreign. Were my rival
my brother only, lady, over his
my rights are sound enough to shield me from
a law that's reasonless. But juster grounds
restrain my claims: I yield to *you,* or, rather,
surrender you the place and scepter which
your sires received in great Erechtheus' line.[28]

---

[28] *To avoid excessive detail in the stage presentation I omitted
Racine's next line, which says: "Ægeus procured the scepter*

Though Athens, wide-extended and protected
by Theseus, welcomed once with joy my father
as King, and thus consigned your luckless brothers
to base oblivion, now Athens calls
you back within her ramparts; she has groaned
enough from this long strife; her fields are glutted
with blood of yours which made the meadows reek,
the soil whence sprang that blood. I rule in Troezen.
The lands of Crete afford a rich retreat
for Phaedra's son. All Athens is yours. I leave
to join the suffrages divided now,
and make them one—for *you*.

    ARICIA: I am confused—
astounded by your words; I fear almost—
I fear I am deluded by a dream!
    [*With a touch of coquetry*]
Am I in truth awake? Dare I believe
your purpose? Oh, my lord, what high divinity
inspires your breast? How justly is your fame
spread everywhere, on every tongue! How much
the truth exceeds report! Would you, for me,
betray your dearest interests? Have you
already not been generous enough
in never having hated me?—in having long
forbidden enmity a harbor in
your bosom?

---

    through adoption." Ægeus, *father of Theseus, was himself said
to be only the adopted son of Pandion, King of Athens; Pallas,
father of Aricia, was the legitimate son. Hence the revolt of
Aricia's brothers when the succession fell to Theseus.*—B.D.N.G.

HIPPOLYTUS: [*The wounded lover*]
　　　　　　Enmity? And hate? For you,
my lady? Dark though were the colors which
my pride's been painted, was it possible
you deemed a monster bore me in her womb?
What savage ways, what hardened hate could fail
to be assuaged to sweetness in your presence?
And how was I to hope withstand the spell
beguiling of—?
　　[*He halts on the verge of declaring his passion*]
　　ARICIA: [*Encouragingly*]
　　　　　　Of what, my lord?
　　HIPPOLYTUS: [*The dam breaking*]
　　　　　　　　　　　　　　I am
too deep plunged into this to halt! My mind—
I see that reason drowns in passion's torrent!
Then since I have begun to shatter silence,
my lady, I shall follow through. I must
make known to you a secret which my heart
no longer can envelop close.
　　[*In surrender*]
　　　　　　　　　　　　Here stands
a wretched prince, example everlasting
of outrageous arrogance. I, so long
in proud revolt against love's laws, so long
a mocker of those chained in love's iron fetters—
yes, I who wept the shipwreck of weak men
and thought to watch the tempests, always safe,
from shore, am now by universal law
of love subjected too!

[*In happy anguish*]

With what distress
I find me swept away far off from all
I thought myself to be! One instant saw
my rash assurance overcome; my soul,
so haughty once, at last is humbled.

[*With exaltation*]

Since
some six months past, ashamed and desperate,
wearing where I go the arrow which
has rent me, I engage in futile struggle
against myself and you. Yes, where you are
I flee; and where you are not, there I seek
to find you; in the depths of woods your image
is at my heels; the light of day, the dark
of night—all trace again before my eyes
the beauty I avoid—all things unite
to render to your hands Hippolytus
the rebel. I myself, as all the fruit
of my inept precautions, search myself
and find myself no longer.

[*More impetuously*]

Javelin
and bow, my chariot—are but a plague
to me. I have forgotten Neptune's teaching;
my groans alone re-echo through the forests;
my flying coursers hear no more my voice,
would know its sound no more.

[*He turns to her*]

Perhaps this tale

of love, so barbarous, will make you blush
to hear me speak your handiwork. What rude
expression does this heart of mine employ
in offering you itself! How strange this captive
in your lovely bonds!

[*Tenderly*]

But the offering,
I think, should be the dearer to your eyes:
for think, how strangely comes this language to
my tongue! Do not reject my passion that
it is so ill-expressed! Hippolytus,
if not for you, could not have framed these words.

Act II
Scene 3

[*Enter* THERAMENES]

THERAMENES: My lord, the Queen approaches.

I have just
passed by her. She is seeking you.

HIPPOLYTUS: Me?

THERAMENES: I do not know her purpose. She has sent
to ask for you.

[*Significantly*]

Before you take your leave
Queen Phaedra would have audience with you.

HIPPOLYTUS: Queen Phaedra? What am I to say to her?
Can she expect—?

ARICIA: [*Charitably*]

My lord, you cannot well
refuse to hear her. Though convinced she is
your enemy, you owe her tears some shade
of pity.

[*She looks at him with love, and starts to move off*]

HIPPOLYTUS: [*Drawing her by the arm to him*]
        And will you leave me thus? And thus
am I to go, not knowing if I have
offended the beauty I adore?—not knowing
if left in your fair hands, this heart of mine—?
    ARICIA: Now go, my prince; and follow up your noble
intentions. Render Athens tributary
to my dominion.
    [*Reassuringly*]
                I accept *each* gift
you wish to make me;
    [*Moving*]
                        but indeed that high
and glorious command of empire I
hold not the dearest of your gifts to *me*.
    [*Exeunt* ARICIA *and* ISMENE]   II : 4
    HIPPOLYTUS: [*Impetuously*]
My friend, is all in readiness?
    [*Looking off*]
                        Alas,
I see the Queen approaches. Go and order
that everyone be prompt for our departure
with speed. Give you the signal and command—
haste back at once to liberate me from
an interview that's bound to vex me much.
    [*Exit* THERAMENES. *Enter* PHAEDRA *and* OENONE]
    PHAEDRA: [*To* OENONE]
He's here. Back to my heart my blood flows off.
I have forgot, in seeing him, the words
I came to tell him.

Act II
sne 4

ne 5

Act II Scene 5
Imitated from
Seneca

Phi. avowal of love to Hipp.— one of the two
great scenes in the play. The other is Phi.
confession of love to the nurse, Act I, Sc. 3

[*She moves to go out*]

OENONE: [*Whispering fiercely*]

Think then of your son,
whose only hope is you.

PHAEDRA: [*Approaches* HIPPOLYTUS, *fumbling for words*]
I hear you will
depart at once and place a distance between
us, my good lord.

[*Hesitant*]   I come to add my tears
of grief to yours. I come to tear aside
for you the veils that hide my fears.

[*In a choked voice*]

My son
no longer owns a father; soon will come
the day that witnesses *my* death as well.
Already enemies by hundreds threat
his childhood. You alone could take up his
defense against them. Secretly remorse
disturbs my heart: I fear I've closed your ears
to his entreaties. I have cause to dread
your righteous anger sate itself on him
because you hate his mother.

HIPPOLYTUS: [*Politely*]

Lady, I
have never cherished sentiments so low.

PHAEDRA: [*With more confidence*]
If you do hate me, I dare not complain,
my lord. You've seen me consecrated to
your injury. You could not read my heart
of hearts, however. I have taken care

to win myself your animosity;
I would not suffer that the land I dwelt
in shelter you. In public, as in secret,
I spoke against you, strove to put vast seas
between us. I indeed forbade by law
your name to be pronounced before my face.

[*A pause; then piteously*]

If, none the less, the punishment is meted
according to the crime—if hate alone
can draw your hatred—never was a woman
more worthy pity—or less worthy hate,
my lord, than I.

HIPPOLYTUS: [*Placatingly, not understanding her*]
                    A mother jealous of
her children's rights will rarely pardon, lady,
the son born to another wife, I know.
Suspicions endless and vexatious are
the common fruits of second marriages.
Sure, any other would have taken like
offense against me; I indeed might well
have suffered greater outrages than yours.

PHAEDRA: Ah no, my lord! I swear that Heaven has
exempted me from *such* behavior!

[*Turning away from him; slowly*]
                              Far,
far different has been the care that vexes
my peace, that now devours me!

HIPPOLYTUS: [*Making an effort to comfort her*]
                            My lady,
this is no time to agitate yourself.

Perhaps your husband still beholds the light;
perhaps the Heavens answering our tears
will give him back to us. For Neptune is
his guardian, and my father would not seek
in vain that god's protection.

PHAEDRA: [*Dully*]

Not twice—no man
can visit twice the banks where dwell the dead,
my lord. Since Theseus now inhabits those
sad somber shores, all hope is vain a god
can send him you again. For Acheron
is greedy and will never loose its prey.

[*With a sudden lift of voice, her feelings mastering her*]
What say I? Theseus is *not* dead—he breathes
in you. Before my very eyes I seem
to see my spouse—I see him, speak to him—.
My heart—

[*Desperately*]

I'm lost, my lord!

[*Looking away; more to herself than to him*]

Despite myself
my foolish passion will unmask itself!

HIPPOLYTUS: [*With pity*]
Astounding are the fruits of your devotion,
I see; and dead though Theseus is, he's here
before your eyes; your soul in love of him
must ever be a scorching fire.

PHAEDRA: [*At last looking straight at him*]

Yes,
I long, I burn for Theseus, prince. I love

him, not as dwellers of the infernal shades
have seen him, fickle worshiper of myriad
successive loves, who vilified the couch
of Hades' deity himself—ah no!
but faithful, proud, yes even fiercely proud—

[*With increasing tenderness*]

yet charming too, and young, attracting hearts
of all beholders, as only Gods are said
to do—or as I now behold in you.

[*Eagerly*]

He had your very bearing—yes, your eyes,
your trick of speech—he wore that noble blush
that colored his fair skin—when he traversed
the seas to Crete and by his worth aroused
my sister's love[29]—mine too, alas! Ah what
were you that time about? And why should he
have summoned all the finest heroes Greece
could boast,

[*With love*]

                without Hippolytus? And why
were you too young then to have sailed aboard
the vessel when it brought him to our shores?
You might have been the one whose sword had slain
the Minotaur, despite the windings of
his vast retreat.[30]

[*With increasing passion*]

                That you might win your way
through its uncertain turns, my sister would

---

[29] *Ariadne's.*
[30] *the labyrinth where the Minotaur was housed.*

have armed your hand with that same fateful thread.[31]
But no! For I'd have been before her with
my help! It's I, not Ariadne, love
would first have taught that care of you!

[*In a rush of passion*]

                                        It's I

my prince, I know it's I whose aid would out
that winding labyrinth have shown you the
escape! Solicitude for your dear head
had been my sought and cherished task! No thread
could then have satisfied your lover's fears;
a sharer of the peril you were doomed
to face, I would have walked before you to
encounter it myself. Within that maze
I would have penetrated by your side,
and chosen by your side to have emerged
or by your side within that maze to perish!

HIPPOLYTUS: [*Shocked*]

Great Gods! What's this I hear? My lady, can
you have forgot that Theseus is my father?—
that Theseus is your husband?

PHAEDRA: [*In confusion, trying to recover her dignity*]

                                Why do you

infer I have forgotten, prince? or that
I've lost all sense of caring for my honor?

HIPPOLYTUS: [*Glad of an excuse to leave*]

---

[31] *by means of which Ariadne helped Theseus find his way out of
the labyrinth after the hero had slain the Minotaur. Without
that aid Theseus would have wandered lost among its mazes until
he perished.*

My lady, pray forgive me. Though I blush
to own it, I had misconstrued your words
and all their innocence. My shame thereat
cannot sustain your glance another moment.
I go—

   [*Starts to leave*]

   PHAEDRA: [*Restraining him. It is useless
to pretend further*]

      Ah, cruel man! You understood
my words too well! I've said too much to draw
you into error! Alas, alas! Now hear
what Phaedra is and all her madness! I—
I love you.

   [HIPPOLYTUS *tries to speak; she intercepts him, rapidly*]

      Think not at the moment when
I love you that I fail to feel my guilt,
or that I like myself for loving you—
nor deem my weak compliance nourishes
the poison of this maddening love which so
unseats my reason! I, unhappy victim
of vengeful gods, abhor myself far more
than you could possibly detest me. I
can call upon the Gods to witness that!—
those Gods who lit the fatal fire in
my body, burning in my veins—those Gods
whose cruel sport it is to lead astray
a feeble woman's heart!

   [*He turns from her in growing horror*]

                    Yourself, recall

to mind the past! It was not enough for me
to flee you, cruel one—I chased you from
the land! I sought to seem inhuman, hateful—
the better to resist you I besought
your hatred. What availed my idle efforts?
You hated me the more—I loved you none
the less. And my injustices to you
but lent you new enchantment. Languishing,
I withered—now in flames, and now in tears—
your eyes must sure persuade you this is truth—
if but your eyes one moment deigned to look
at me. Alas! What am I saying!

[*With self-loathing!*]

                                            Can
you think that this avowal which I've made—
this vile avowal—can you think I made
it willingly?

[HIPPOLYTUS *covers his ears with his hands, to hear
no more*]

                        I came to beg you not
to hate my son, for whom I tremble, and
whose safety I must not betray. How weak
the purpose of a heart that is too full
of what it loves! Alas! of you alone
can I find words to speak!

[*With violence*]

                                    Revenge yourself!
Now punish swift this odious love I hold!
You are a worthy son to that great hero
who gave you birth—then free the world of such

a loathsome beast as she who thus offends
you.

[*With irony*]

   Theseus' widow dares to love his son!
Believe me, never let your arm release
this shocking monster free.

[*Tearing at her robe, baring her breast*]

                  Here! Here's my heart.

[*She clutches his arm*]

Here let your hand deal swift the blow. I feel
it anxious now to expiate its sin—
I feel it pressing forth to meet your arm!

[*In a frenzy*]

Strike, strike! Or if perhaps you deem it too
unworthy of your stroke—if punishment
so sweet your hate begrudges me—or if
your hand would shrink from being steeped in blood
so utterly polluted,

[*With sudden violence*]

                lend me then—
if not your arm, your sword. Quick, lend me it!

[*She pulls out his sword from its sheath and tries to stab
herself.* OENONE *rushes to her, and hurries her away*]

OENONE: What are you doing, lady? Gods above!—
Quick, someone comes! Avoid a meeting in
this state. Go in, come quick!—or else you're shamed!

[OENONE *grasps the sword from her as she and* PHAEDRA
hurriedly exeunt. HIPPOLYTUS *stands dazed. Enter*
THERAMENES]

THERAMENES: Is that Queen Phaedra fleeing?—

should I say

is that she being dragged away?—

[*Walking towards him*]

What mean

these signs of sorrow, lord?—What's happened to
your sword? Why are you thus abashed?—and pale?

HIPPOLYTUS: [*Moving*]

Good Theramenes, let us flee. I'm shocked
beyond the telling you. I could not face
myself without revulsion—Phaedra—

[*He is about to confide in him; then changes his mind*]

No!

Great Gods! Entomb that dreadful secret in
oblivion without an end!

THERAMENES: If you
are ready to depart, the sails are up.
But Athens, lord, already has declared
itself. Her leaders know the votes of all
the people. Phaedra wins. Your brother's chosen.

HIPPOLYTUS: [*Bitterly*]

She wins?

THERAMENES:

A herald bearing Athens' voice
has come to place the kingdom's reins within
her hands. Her son is King, my noble lord.

HIPPOLYTUS: You Gods who know her! Can you

thus requite

her virtue?

THERAMENES:

      None the less it's darkly rumored
your royal father still is with the living,
that in Epirus Theseus has been seen—
but I who sought him there—I know alas!—

    HIPPOLYTUS: [*Eagerly*]

Yet even so, we must neglect no hope.
Let us investigate this rumor, trace
it to its source. If it should merit no
delaying of my voyage, let us leave.
Whatever price we pay, let us at least
confer the rule on hands deserving it.

    [*Exeunt*]

ACT THREE

Scene 1

[PHAEDRA *and* OENONE *are alone*]

PHAEDRA: Let them bestow elsewhere the honors brought me.

[*She sits on the chair*]

Why do you persist in urging me
to see them? What's your new design to flatter
my desolated spirits? Rather hide
me from the world. I've spoken far too much.
The madness of my love has overflowed
its banks; I've uttered words that he should not
have ever heard. O heavens! How he heard
them! By how many cold evasions did
he seek to find escape from what I meant!
How eagerly he hoped but for a quick
retreat! And how his blushes but redoubled
the shame I felt! Why did you turn my thoughts
away from my desire for death? Alas!
When at my breast his sword was pointed, did
he pale the least, or did he wrest it from
my hands? Because my hands had touched it once
I rendered it repugnant to his touch—
the wretched sword would now profane his grasp—

OENONE: If you refuse to think of nothing but
your misery, you'll only nourish fire
which you must quench. Were it not worthier
the blood of Minos[32] if you sought your peace

---

[32] *Phaedra's father, King of Crete.*

46

in nobler undertakings—and to spite
an ingrate who prefers to run from you,
to rule, and shoulder the affairs of state?

PHAEDRA: [*Ironically*]

I rule?

[*Rising*]

I rule the state? Enforce my laws?
When my enfeebled reason cannot sway
my own behavior? When I've given up
control of my own senses? When I scarce
can breathe beneath this leaden yoke of shame?
and dying—?

OENONE: Fly.

PHAEDRA: I dare not leave him.

OENONE: Once
you dared to banish him! Yet now you dare
not leave—

PHAEDRA:

Too late for that! He knows my mad
obsession. I have passed beyond the bounds
of decent modesty. I've shown my shame
before my victor's eyes. Yet hope, despite
my will, usurps my heart. And you, yourself,
recalled my failing powers:

[*She moves to columns slowly*]

                              life upon
my lips was trembling to depart when your
deceiving counsel coaxed it back; you made
it seem that I might love him.

[*Her voice indicates a rebirth of hope*]

OENONE: Oh, alas!
if I *be* innocent or guilty of
your sorrows, what was I not capable
of compassing to save you? But if slights
have power to irritate your spirit, can
you overlook this haughty man's contempt?
How cruel were his eyes when he beheld
you nearly prostrate at his feet—and he
obdurately inhuman! His disdain
seemed barbarous, his arrogance disgusting!
That moment why could you not see him with
my eyes?

[*Phaedra moves slowly up the steps, leans against a column*]

PHAEDRA: Oenone dear, his pride which wounds
you thus, might die yet. Bred in forests, he
has naturally their roughness. He, remember,
was toughened under savage principles;
mine was his earliest experience
of words of love.

[*She throws her arms behind her around the column, supporting herself in this way; she speaks caressingly*]
                    Perhaps astonishment
might cause such silence; it may be my pleas
were far too violent.

OENONE: Do not forget
a savage mother gave him birth.

PHAEDRA: Although
a Scythian and savage, none the less

she learned to love.

OENONE: He holds for every woman
unswerving loathing.

PHAEDRA: Then I need not fear
a rival taking precedence of me.

[*Walking slowly*]
Your counsel's altogether out of season—
you must perceive that!

[*With a sudden rush of enthusiasm, she walks rapidly
to* OENONE *and presses her to her*]
                        Serve my *folly*, then,
Oenone, not my sanity. If he
opposes love with such a hardened heart,
let us discover a more feeling place
to level love's attack. Perhaps the charms
of kingship may prove tempting. Athens draws
him there—he has admitted that. Already
his vessels' prows are pointed to her shores;
their loosened sails are wafted to the wind.

[*Commandingly*]
For love of me, go find the ambitious youth,
Oenone, make the crown to glitter in
his eyes. Yes, let the sacred diadem
bedeck *his* brow, and for myself I ask
no greater honor than to fix it there.
I yield to him the power I cannot keep.

[*Convincing herself that she can attain his love*]
He shall instruct my son the art of ruling;
perhaps he will be willing to become

his father by adoption. I shall place
both son and mother under his protection.

[*Entreatingly*]

Use every means to bend him. You shall find
more readily the words to move him than
can I. Lament and weep, persuade him. Stir
up his compassion for the anguished Phaedra.
Nor blush at all to play the suppliant.
I shall approve of all you'll do. You are
my only hope. Now go. I wait for your
return to learn if I must live or die.

[*Exit* OENONE, *shaking her head in doubt*]

Act III
Scene 2

[*Kneeling*]

O you who see the shame to which I have
descended!

[*Clasping her hands*]

      Venus, am I not enough
confounded? Surely you cannot protract
your cruelty much further! All your shafts
have hit their mark! O cruel goddess, if
you need a newer triumph, strike a foe
who's ever been your rebel! Hippolytus
has shunned you, braved your wrath, and never at
your altars bent his knees. Your very name
would seem to wound his scornful ears. O goddess!
avenge yourself! Your cause and mine are one!
Then make him love—.

[*Looking off, she rises in consternation*]

      Already you return,
Oenone? He detests me! He'll not hear you!

Act III Scene 3

[*Re-enter* OENONE]

OENONE: My lady, you must stifle every thought
of this unfruitful love. Recall to you
your former virtue. Theseus, whom report
made dead, will soon appear before your eyes.

[PHAEDRA *staggers to the chair to support herself*]
My lady, Theseus has arrived; he's *here*.
The people throng in eagerness to see him.
I went as you commanded, sought his son—
when suddenly a thousand cries rose up—

PHAEDRA: [*In a dead voice*]
My husband is alive, Oenone. You
have said enough. I've made a vile avowal
of love dishonoring him. He is alive.
I wish to know of nothing further—

OENONE: What?

PHAEDRA: [*Crushed*]
I did predict it; you refused to have
it so. Your tears prevailed despite my own
compunctions. Had I died this day I might
have earned a name of virtue. Because of you
I die dishonored.

OENONE: Die?

PHAEDRA: [*In terror*]
                    Just Heaven! What
have I today accomplished? Theseus will
appear—with him his son. I must behold
the witness of my criminality
observe with what effrontery I dare
to greet his father, heart surcharged with sighs

he would not hear, and eyes suffused with tears
he stolidly repulsed. You think he will
conceal from Theseus, from consideration
of Theseus' honor, my devouring passion?
Will he allow himself betrayal both
of King and sire? Can he restrain perforce
the horror that he feels for me? It were
a futile hope he could keep silence. My
own breach of faith I know; I'm none of those
bold women who can taste tranquility
of mind while sinning, and can muster calm
without a blush. I know my madness; all
of it suffuses me.

[*Shrinking from her thoughts*]

                              I feel as if
these walls, these vaulted ceilings, are prepared
to speak, Oenone, ready to accuse
me, waiting for my spouse to undeceive
his trust in me . . . Die I must.

[*She sinks into the couch*]

                              Let death
deliver me from all this horror! Can
it be so great an ill to cease to live?
No, death can cause no terror to the wretched.
I only dread the name I leave behind—
what bitter heritage for my poor sons!
The blood of Jupiter[33] should swell their hearts

---

[33] *Minos, Phaedra's father, was descended from Zeus (the Roman
name: Jupiter).*

with pride; whatever pride might raise so fine
a lineage, their mother's sin must weigh
them down, a heavy burden. Evil talk—
alas, how merited!—I dread, hereafter
must be their lot—reproach to them for all
their mother's guilt. I fear beneath that loathsome
indictment, neither boy will ever dare
to look upon the world—

    OENONE: I pity them—
you know that.

   [*With emphasis*]

              Never fear had juster grounds.
Then why expose them to such insults? Why
become your own accuser? People will
be bound to say that Phaedra was too full
of guilt to face the formidable sight
of Theseus, the husband she betrayed. You die—
Hippolytus rejoices that your death
lends weight to what he charges. Then what could
Oenone answer your accusers? He
will easily confound my words, and I
should see him revel in his horrid triumph,
recount your shame to all who'd lend an ear.
Ah, rather let the lightning strike me dead!

   [*Abruptly*]

Tell me: now how do you hold that prince?

    PHAEDRA: A monster dreadful for my eyes to see!

    OENONE: Why grant him then entire victory?
You fear him. Be the first to bring the charge
of sin which he may level at any time

against your peace. Who'll contradict your stand?
All things belie his tale. His sword which luck
left in your hands—your present troubles and
your past unhappiness—his father warned
long since by your insistent cries—his exile
procured by you already—

   PHAEDRA: Do you think
I'd dare defame and slander innocence?

   OENONE: From you my task requires nothing but
your silence. Faint of heart as you, I feel
revulsion at the task: you'd see me prompt
to sooner face for you a thousand deaths.
But since without this painful cure I lose
my mistress,

  [*Pleadingly*]

             dearer is your life to me
than any price I pay. *I'll* speak. The King,
incensed by what I'll say, will limit vengeance
to exile for his son. A father, sure,
when punishing is still a father. He
will sate his wrath without severity.
But even though his guiltless blood *he* shed,
does not your menaced reputation ask
protection? That's a treasure far too dear
to compromise. Expedience is needed;
you must submit, my lady; and to shield
your honor from attack you must prepare
to sacrifice all things—yes, even virtue.

  [*Trumpet offstage; she looks offstage, and moves to the
other side of* PHAEDRA]

They come. I see the King—

PHAEDRA: [*Rising*]

Hippolytus

I see. His insolent expression shows
my ruin. Do your will, I yield to you.
With all this woe, I can do nothing well.

[*Enter* THESEUS, HIPPOLYTUS, *and* THERAMENES] *Act III Scene*

THESEUS: [*Standing between columns*]

My lady, Fortune wars no more against
my wishes.

[*He moves a little*]

She restores me to your arms—

[*Attempting to embrace her*]

PHAEDRA: [*Escaping his embrace*]

Cease, cease! Do not profane a rapture so
endearing, Theseus!

[*Looking away from him*]

I no longer earn
such words of sweet affection. You are wronged.
Malevolence of fate has spared your wife
nothing while you, her lord, were absent. I'm
no longer fit to come near you or to
be pleasing in your eyes. I must not hope
henceforth beyond the hope to hide from you.

[*Exeunt* PHAEDRA *and* OENONE]   *Act III Scene 5*

THESEUS: What is this strange reception that they give
your father, son?

HIPPOLYTUS: This mystery no one
but Phaedra can explain . . .

[*Steps forward with gesture of supplication*]

                                    If urgent prayer
can move you, sir, allow me never more
to see her. Suffer that your fearful son
may quit the habitation of your wife
forever.

   THESEUS: You, my son, to run from me?

   HIPPOLYTUS: *I* did not seek her. *You* it was who brought
her to these shores. You deigned, my lord, when you
departed, to entrust Aricia and
the Queen to Troezen's lands, and charged me with
the duty of their safety. Now what care
for them need henceforth keep *me* here? My youth
has idled years enough in proving skill
against *unvalued* enemies which dwell
in forests. It is time to change this shameful
inactive life; may I not stain with blood
more glorious my javelins?

   [*With youthful excitement*]

                              When you
had not yet reached my age, much more than one
proud tyrant, more than one wild beast had felt
the weight of your strong arm; already you
had rendered safe the shores of two vast seas,
a joyous victor over threatening men
of violence; the traveler was free
and feared no further outrage; Hercules
more easy breathed on hearing your exploits,[34]

---

[34] *According to Plutarch Theseus began to fight the robbers when
Hercules was in servitude for three years to Omphale, Queen of
Lydia.*

and ceased his labors, confident that you
could well relieve him. I, the unknown son
of so illustrious a father—I
am far behind the footsteps even of
my mother. Suffer me to give my courage
the room to *find* itself. Perhaps there lives
some monster overlooked by you—perhaps
I'll win the noble spoils and lay them at
your feet. Else let the lasting memory
of death won honorably eternize
the name of one whose days made noble end,
and prove to all the world I *was* your son.

    THESEUS: [*With rising wrath*]
What's this I find? What horror's overspread
this land to make my family distract
and fleeing from my eyes? If I return
so feared, so little wished for, why, O Gods,
did you release me from my prison? I
but owned one friend.[35] His reckless passion sought
the wife to ravish of Epirus' tyrant;[36]
reluctantly I served his amorous
designs; but incensed fate did blind us both:
the king surprised me all defenseless, with
no arms. With tears I saw Pirithoüs
delivered horribly to cruel beasts

---

[35] *Pirithoüs.*

[36] *Plutarch assigns a different end to Pirithoüs from the one we have already mentioned. The king mentioned in this exploit is said by Plutarch to have thrown the hero to his dogs to be eaten alive by them.*

by that barbarian, who fed them blood
of mortal men, his victims. He penned me
in gloomy caverns deep beneath the ground,
near where the shades infernal dwell. The Gods
when six months passed, at last took pity on me.
I found the way to cheat the eyes of them
who guarded me, and purged the world of a
perfidious wretch; I served himself as food
to his foul monsters. When with rapture I
believed myself returning home to all
the Gods have granted dearest to my soul—
What say I? When my hungered soul is panting
to glut itself, to feed in rapture on
those cherished sights, my only welcome is
a shuddering fear! Everyone escapes
and everyone rejects my longed embrace!

[*Bitterly*]

And I, because of all the terror I
inspire, now wish me back in prison at
Epirus!

[*Angrily*]

      Speak! The Queen complains I have
been wronged. Who's my betrayer?

[HIPPOLYTUS *begins to speak, but turns away*]

                        Why am I
revenged not? Greece too many times has found
my arm of use to her; does Greece afford
asylum to the criminal?

[*He waits for a reply*]

            You're silent!

[*Walking toward him*]

My son, flesh of my flesh,

    [*Pointing an accusing finger at him*]

                          are you allied

with enemies of mine? . . .

    [HIPPOLYTUS *is silent*]

                       I'll go within.

This overwhelming doubt must be resolved.

I'll hear at once the criminal and crime.

Let Phaedra tell the grief I find her in.

    [*Exit* THESEUS]

    HIPPOLYTUS: [*Too innocent to imagine that he could be*   Act III Scene 6

victimized, pitying PHAEDRA *and his father*]

What signified her words, which freeze with fear

my soul? Will Phaedra, prey of wildest madness

accuse herself, be executioner

to her own safety? Gods! How will the King

reply?

    [*Thinking of* ARICIA, *he almost sympathizes with*

PHAEDRA's *plight*]

        What mortal poison love has spread

throughout this house!

    [*Putting a hand on* THERAMENES' *shoulder*]

                  Myself inflamed with love

his hate forbids—how different the son

he knew from him he finds on his return!

I am engulfed by black forebodings. But

I'm sure that innocence has naught to fear.

    [*Thinking only of his love for* ARICIA]

I'll go seek elsewhere by what lucky skill

I may evoke my father's tenderness,
and tell him of the love he'll wish perhaps
to thwart, but all his might can never kill.

    [*Exeunt*]

ACT FOUR

Scene 1

[*Enter* THESEUS, *furious, making long strides, followed by* OENONE]

THESEUS: What's this I hear? That reckless traitor was
not loath to violate his father's honor?
O Destiny, with what relentlessness
do you pursue me! Where I go I know not,
nor where I am. My love for him—my bounty—
how ill repaid they are! Audacious plot!

[*Covering his eyes with his arm as if to blot out the foul image*]

Revolting image! To gain the end of his
nefarious love, the scoundrel did not scruple
to borrow violence! I know the sword,
the instrument of his mad passion. *I*
once armed him with that blade for nobler deeds!
Could not the bonds of blood restrain his rage?
And what of Phaedra? Dares she hesitate
to have the villain punished? Is it sign
that she would spare him that she keeps her silence?

OENONE: No! Phaedra rather spares his father, whose
position is so pitiable. She's
humiliated that the passion of
a lover so depraved, so criminal,
should be evoked by her. She wished to die;
with murderous hand, indeed, would have put out
the light of her eyes' innocence that could

61

ignite such love. I saw her raise her arm,
and ran to save her; I alone, evoking
your love of her, preserved her life. Compassion
for both her sorrow and your shock compels
me to explain aright her tears to you.

THESEUS: That traitor could not help turn pale. I saw
him when we met begin to quake with fear.
I was astounded with how little joy
he greeted me; his cold embraces froze
my tenderness for him.—But tell me, ere
I banished him from Athens, had he yet
declared this passion which destroys him?

OENONE: My lord, remember her complainings. His
corrupting love was father to her hate.

THESEUS: His passion woke anew in Troezen then?

OENONE: [Seeing HIPPOLYTUS approaching]
I've told you all, my lord, that has occurred.
I dare not longer leave the Queen alone
in mortal anguish. I must leave you now.
Permit that I may minister her sorrow.

[Exit OENONE]

Act IV
Scene 2

THESEUS: [Seeing HIPPOLYTUS approaching]
Ah, there he is! Great Gods! What eyes would not
be utterly deceived like mine by his
most noble countenance?

[Love for his son conflicting with hate for the son's deed]
　　　　　　　　　Why must that low
adulterer show radiant on his brow
the sign of every virtue? Why isn't man
forewarned by token that will some way mark

for certain the black heart of the perfidious?

[*He turns away as* HIPPOLYTUS *enters*]

HIPPOLYTUS: [*Innocently*]
What sombre cloud, my lord, can darkly shade
your royal face? Dare I beseech you trust
the secret to my loyal love for you?

THESEUS: You, traitor? Dare you show yourself to me?
Too long have you been spared the lightning shafts,
you monster, vile survivor of the thieves
of whom I've purged the earth! Your horrid lust
could drive you far as to your father's bed—
and yet you dare expose your hated head
to me—dare breathe where all the air is charged
with infamy of yours!

[HIPPOLYTUS *silently supplicates his father's
understanding but* THESEUS' *fury pours on*]
                        You do not run
to seek beneath some unknown sky a land
where Theseus' name is yet unheard of?

[*With a gesture, exiling him*]

                                    Fly,
you traitor! Do not dare to brave my hate
within this place, nor tempt a wrath I scarce
restrain! Enough of shame eternal that
I fathered so depraved a son, without
blame adding to my memory your death
to taint the glory of my noble deeds!

[*His hand grasping his sword, without drawing it*]
Then, fly! Unless you wish a sudden stroke
may join you with the rascals punished by

this arm, take care that never shall this sun
whose beams now give us light, behold you tread
securely rash this soil! Now, fly, I say!
Return no more, make haste! And see you rid
my empire of your noxious face!

   [*Arms uplifted to the Gods*]

                              And you,
O Neptune, you, if ever I have cleansed
your shores of base assassins, do you recall
your promise to repay my lucky efforts
by granting me my first of prayers! Long
confined in cruel prison, I have never
implored the help of your immortal power;
for niggard of your help, I kept my prayers
until I had the greatest need. Today
I do beseech your aid! A wretched father
asks vengeance!

   [*He points an accusing arm at his son, who turns away to
hide his face from his father*]

                     Extinguish in his blood
his brazen-faced desires! By your wrath
shall Theseus recognize your bounty to him!

   HIPPOLYTUS: I am accused by Phaedra of a love
unlawful! This excessive horror stuns
my soul. These many unexpected blows
at once, cut off my speech and choke my voice.

   THESEUS: You hoped that Phaedra would in

                             coward silence
keep buried, wretch, your brutal insolence!
Then you should not have left your sword with her

as evidence against you when you fled—
or rather, should have crowned your treachery
with one fell stroke that robbed her of her speech.

HIPPOLYTUS: So black a lie might justly make me hot
to tell the truth, my lord; but I suppress
the secret touching close your honor. If
my lips are sealed, commend my reverence.
I do not seek you should augment your woes—
[*Stepping towards his father*]
but think you what my life has been, and what
I am. Great crimes are wont to follow on
the heels of lesser crimes. Who breaks the law
will end by violating sacred ties,
for crime, like virtue, has its own degrees.
There is no man has ever yet beheld
shy innocence become extremest vice
in one quick move. One day will not suffice
to turn a virtuous man to murderer,
or traitor cowardly incestuous.
A breast heroic, chaste, it was, which gave
me suck. I never yet belied my blood.
I do not wish to paint myself in boastful
portrayal, but allow some share to me
of virtue, father, and concede I've shown
most notably abhorrence of those crimes
imputed now to me. Hippolytus
is known for nothing else through all of Greece.
I've kept my chastity to point of rudeness.
[*Manfully*]
All know my rigorous austerity.

The day's not clearer than my inmost heart.
Could you suppose that I'd profane with passion—?
   THESEUS: Yes, coward! You're condemned by
                              that same pride!
I see the odious meaning of your coldness.
It's Phaedra who alone bewitched your lustful
desires! Callous to all innocence,
your soul disdained the fires of other loves.
   HIPPOLYTUS: No, father. I've concealed the truth
                                 too long:
[*He imagines, in his youth, that the moment is propitious
to reveal his love for* ARICIA]
my heart has not disdained chaste love's desires.
   [*He kneels*]
Here at your feet I do confess my true
offense.
   [*Seeing his son on his knees,* THESEUS *is moved to
tenderness, makes as if to touch the boy's head, but
withdraws his hand in renewed anger as he hears*
ARICIA'S *name*]
        I love. I love, it's true, despite
your prohibition. It is *Aricia*
to whom my heart is bound. Your son is vanquished
by Pallas' daughter. Rebel to your law
I am; my soul for her alone now burns
and languishes! I worship, I adore
Aricia—!
   THESEUS: Aricia you love?
   [*With sarcasm*]
Good Gods! But no! Your trick is clumsy! You

would feign one crime to justify another!

HIPPOLYTUS: [*Slowly rising*]

My lord, though six months I have shunned her, still
I love her. Trembling, here I came to say
as much to you.

    [*Awaiting a word of understanding*]
                Alas! Can *nothing* draw
you from your misconception? What's the oath
terrific that can reassure your trust?

    [*Attempting a vast oath, in desperation*]

By earth, by all of Nature, and by Heaven—!

THESEUS: A rascal's always prone to perjury.

    [*Bitterly*]

Stop, stop! Spare your importunate avowals,
if your false virtue knows no other help!

HIPPOLYTUS: [*Staunchly*]

It may seem false to you, but Phaedra in
her heart of hearts must be more just to me.

THESEUS: [*Outraged*]

Enough! Your impudence excites my wrath.

HIPPOLYTUS: [*Resigned*]

How long, and where, do you prescribe my exile?

THESEUS: [*With a gesture*]

Beyond the pillars famed of Hercules[37]
you'd still seem far too near, perfidious boy!

HIPPOLYTUS: What friends will pity me, forsaken thus
and charged by you with such a heinous crime?

THESEUS: Go seek for friends who hold in evil honor

---

[37] *Gibraltar, thought by the ancients to be the western limits of the
world.*

adultery, applaud incest, dishonored
betrayers, lawless wretches like yourself,
the fit protectors of a rogue like you!

HIPPOLYTUS: You needs must speak adultery and incest?
[With sudden self-justification]
I'm silent. None the less, you know, my lord,
that Phaedra had a mother—Phaedra comes
of blood these horrors poisoned more than mine!

THESEUS: [Infuriated]
Your rage feels no restraint before my eyes!
For the last time: relieve me of your sight!
Be gone! Don't wait until my ire uproot
you, loathsome traitor, from this land with shame!

[Exit HIPPOLYTUS]

You haste, you wretch, to infallible destruction!
By Styx, the river terrible to Gods
themselves, has Neptune sworn his oath to me,
and must fulfill it. Following your steps
will be a God avenging; him you'll not
escape. I loved you, and despite your crime
my heart is troubled sore for what must yet
befall you. Far too justly you evoked
my curse on you. Did ever son wound father
more deep than you have wounded me? You Gods
who see this sorrow overwhelming me,
could I have sired so culpable a son?

[Enter PHAEDRA]

PHAEDRA: [Pleading]
My lord, I come all quivering with fear.
I heard your terrifying voice afar.

I dread that acts too prompt have made threats good.
If still there's time, oh spare your son! Consider—
your flesh and blood!—I beg of you; have mercy!
    [*A pause.* THESEUS *walks to her protectively*]
Oh save me from the fright—! To hear his blood
cry out from the earth, my lord!—Do not prepare
for me perpetual pain for having moved
his father's hand to shed it!
    THESEUS: No, my lady,
my hand's unstained by blood of his,—but yet
the wretch shall not escape me. Now a power
immortal's master of that traitor's ruin!
You'll be avenged, for Neptune owes it me.
    PHAEDRA: [*Fearful*]
He owes it you? Your prayers breathed in wrath—
    THESEUS: [*Whipping up his anger again*]
What, fear you Neptune will not hearken them?
Then join your pleas with mine. Rehearse for me
his crimes in all their blackness—heat my anger
which is too slow to rise—which yet too much
I do repress. Why, even you know nothing
of all his wickedness's scope! His fury
deluges you with further injuries.
Your tongue, he says, is all deceitfulness,
and he pretends Aricia has his heart,
his faith—that she it is he loves.
    PHAEDRA: [*Stunned*]
                              Aricia?
    THESEUS: He said it to my face. But I repulse
such trumpery and artifice. Let's hope

that Neptune will be swift to wreak him justice.
I'll go myself once more before his altar
to beg fulfillment of his solemn promise.

    [*Exit* THESEUS]

actir Scene 5

    PHAEDRA: He's gone. What new disclosure stuns my ears?
What fire half-stifled in my heart is fanned
again to life! What lightning shafts, O Gods!
What direst tidings!

    [*Sinking into chair*]

                I tore myself away
in terror from Oenone's arms, and rushed
to offer help to poor Hippolytus.
I yielded to remorse, which racks my soul.
Who knows how far repentance might have hurled
my speech?

    [*Reproaching herself*]

          Perhaps I was too willing to
accuse myself. Perhaps, had I not lost
my voice, the terrifying truth might have
been uttered!—

    [*Rising*]

             But Hippolytus *can* feel!—
Hippolytus can feel nothing for me!
Aricia has his heart, his loyalty!
O Gods! When that inexorable ingrate
had armed himself against my pleas with eye
so proud and brow so fearful, I then thought
his heart forever closed to love; I thought
him armed against all women equally.

Another, none the less, can tame his pride!
His cruel eyes saw grace within another!
Perhaps his heart is easily made tender.
I am the only one he cannot bear!
And shall I load myself with his defense?

[*Enter* OENONE]

Act IV Scene 6

Oenone dear, just guess what I have learned!

OENONE: [*Terrified*]
No, no. I come, to tell the truth, with lips
a-tremble, fearful of the plan with which
you sallied forth. I feared you'd take a step
most fatal to yourself—

PHAEDRA: Oenone, who
would once believe it? I have had a rival!

OENONE: A rival?

PHAEDRA: Hippolytus does love—there's no
more room for doubt. That savage enemy
whom none could subjugate, whom my respect
offended, whom my tears but irritated—
that tiger whom I never yet approached
without abasing fear, *can* be subdued—
is *tamed*—acknowledges a *victor!* Yes!
Aricia's found the pathway to his heart.

OENONE: Aricia?

PHAEDRA: Anguish still unsounded! Oh!
What novel torments are reserved for me?
My suffering, my fears, my fits of passion,
the fury of the love I've known, the horror
remorse has brought me—all the injury
intolerable of his cruel rebuff,

were but a feeble foretaste of the torture
I now endure.

   [*With violence*]

               They love! What witchcraft have
they worked to seal my eyes—for I saw nothing?
And how did they contrive to meet? And when?
And where? You must have known! Had you the heart
to let me be deceived? Could you not tell
me of their secret passion? They could not
have failed to be observed when they were meeting
each other. Sure, they must have been observed
in talk! Or was their meeting-place for love
in depths of forests? Alas! Alas for me!
They were full free to see each other! Heaven
approved the innocence of what they felt;
without remorse they followed their desire.
Each day arose serene and clear to *them*.
And I, the outcast of all nature, I
but hid from day—I fled the light—and Death
alone the god I had the courage to
invoke: I waited but the time to die!
I fed on bitterness, was washed with tears,
my misery was all too closely watched—
I dared not let my eyes suffuse with tears
when I had need: that dismal pleasure I
could only taste in fear—beneath serene
calm brow concealing my cruel cares. Too often
I was compelled to cheat myself of tears.

   OENONE: What fruit can they enjoy of futile love
like theirs? They cannot meet another time.

PHAEDRA: [*Turning on her suddenly*]
They'll always love each other. Deadly thought—
this very moment while I speak they can
outface the madness of my adoration!
Though exile now must sunder them, they'll swear
to never part by a thousand tender oaths.
  [*In a frenzy*]
No, no! I cannot tolerate a joy
they purchase by my injury, Oenone!
  [*Clasping her in desperation*]
Oh pity me my jealous rage! We must
undo Aricia! We must revive
my husband's wrath against her hated line!
He must not be content with light restraints;
the sister's crime exceeds the brothers'! While
my fit of jealousy still rules, I'll beg him—.
  [*She makes a gesture of command, then suddenly clasps
her hand over her eyes*]
Alas, alas! What am I thinking now?
Where do my senses stray? I jealous, I?
And Theseus *him* I would implore? My husband
is living—yet I burn. For whom? Whose is
this heart to which *my* scorching heart lays claim?
Each word I utter makes my hair stand up
on end.
  [*In horror at herself*]
        My crimes from this time on exceed
all measure!
  [*With revulsion*]
        I breathe out hypocrisy

and incest every breath. My hands are swift
to seek revenge—are homicidal—ache
to steep themselves in blood of innocents!
Ah wretch! Why do I live? And dare I face
this holy Sun from which I am descended?
I had as ancestor the father and
the king of Gods. The Heavens and the earth
are full of ancestors of mine. Then where
am I to hide? In Hell's infernal night!
Ah no! No! *There* it is my father[38] who
does hold the fatal urn; they say that Fate
has placed it in his hands of justice, Minos
sits judge of all the ghosts of men in Hades.

[*She shields her eyes from the imagined sight*]
Ah! how his terrifying shade will shudder
when he shall see before his eyes his daughter
compelled to make confession of misdeeds
so various—of crimes perhaps unknown
in Hell! What shall you say, my father, at
that loathsome sight? I seem to see you seek
a newer punishment, yourself become
the executioner of your own stock.

[*Imploringly, as though she stood before her father*]
Forgive! A cruel Goddess[39] has destroyed
your family.

[*Beating her breasts*]
                    Behold her vengeance in
the madness of your daughter. Alas, alas!

---

[38] *According to Virgil, Minos was a judge of souls in Hades.*
[39] *(Aphrodite, the Greek Venus).*

My wretched heart has never gathered joy
from that revolting crime whose shame still hounds me!
In torture I give up afflicted life,
pursued till latest breath by misery!

OENONE: Dismiss, my lady, fears so vain as these!
And look more charitably on a weakness
that's pardonable. If you love—you can't
escape your destiny. You were ensnared
by charms that were predestined. Is it such
a prodigy unheard of here? Has love
been victor over no one else but you?
It's but too natural for mortals to
be weak—and being mortal, bear the lot
of mortals. You bemoan a yoke imposed
long since on human frailty. The Gods,
the Gods themselves, the dwellers on Olympus,
who with their terrifying clamor fright
the evil-doer, have themselves sometimes
been singed by illegitimate obsessions.

PHAEDRA: [*Walking to her in denunciation,* OENONE
backing from her advance]
What do you say? What counsel do you give?
Until the very last you wish to spill
your poison in my ears, you wretched woman!
Just so you've ruined me.

[*Pointing an accusing finger;* OENONE *turns away*]
                                        It's you who brought
me back to life when I was ready to
relinquish it. Your pleas made me forget
my duty: you insisted that I see

Hippolytus when I avoided him.
How dared you to presume with wicked tongue
to blacken him with accusations? He
may die for it! The sacrilegious prayer
of his insensate father may be granted!

[OENONE *puts out her arms, half-heartedly, in a plea for understanding.* PHAEDRA *brushes her appeal away*]

I'll hear no more. Away, detestable
and monstrous woman! Go! leave me the weight
of my unenviable fate! And may
just Heaven pay you back in full as you

[*With increasing fury*]

deserve! And may your punishment strike fear
forever into those who, just as you,
by wicked artifice give nourishment
to weaknesses of luckless princes—push
them to the chasm where their hearts invite them—
and smoothe the road to crime! Pernicious, vile—
you flatterers, the direst gift the wrath
of Heaven can bestow upon a monarch!

[*Exit*]

OENONE: Oh Gods! To serve her I have given all,
relinquished all! And this is my reward—
and this the thanks I have deserved from her?

[*Exit*]

ACT FIVE

Scene 1

[*Enter* ARICIA *followed by* HIPPOLYTUS. *He is far too happy over the prospect of being joined to her to be troubled by his situation. During* ARICIA'S *first speech,* ISMENE *enters quietly and remains*]

ARICIA: In this extremest danger are you silent?
and leave a father who so loves you, lost
in error?

[*She turns away from him to hide her feelings. He beams his love for her*]

      Reckless man, if you misprize
my tears and can consent with ease to see
me never more, then go! Then place a distance
between yourself and sad Aricia.

[*Turning to him again*]

But when you go at least make safe your life.
Defend your honor from the brand of shame,
and force your father to revoke his vows.
There still is time. Oh why, by what caprice
can you desert the field to your accuser?
Make Theseus know—

HIPPOLYTUS: [*Interrupting her*]

      My words mean nothing, then?
Should I have glaringly exposed the shame
done to this bed? Should I have told too true
a tale, and made my father's brow glow red
at the disgrace? This secret odium

77

you have alone unearthed. My heart reveals
itself to none but you and Heaven. I
could not conceal—then judge how I love you—
from you what I would fain conceal from me
myself. Remember under what dread seal
of secrecy it was revealed to you.
Forget what I have said—

   [*Bitterly*]

                        if but you can
forget, my lady. Never let two lips
so pure as yours be severed to relate
that horrifying act. Let's trust the Gods
to deal out justice; they must be concerned
enough in this to clear me. Phaedra for
her crime will soon or late be punished—she
shall not avoid the ignominy she
has earned. It is the sole request I make:
but for the rest I give my rage full range.

   [*Impetuously going to her*]
Escape the slavery to which you are
reduced; take courage, leave with me—be brave!
Let's fly together, love, and wrest yourself
from this profaned and baneful place where goodness
must breathe in poisoned air. Make use of what
confusion my disgrace provokes to cover
your swift departure. I'll secure the means.
For powerful defenders shall become
our partisans. Stout Argos and strong Sparta
will lend their arms to us. Let's bear our griefs
to common friends, nor suffer Phaedra gather

what yet remains to us of shattered fortune,
and hunt us both from our paternal throne,
and hope to robe her son with spoils from us.
Occasion offers—
    [ARICIA *moves away gently in confusion. A pause*]
               we must now embrace it.
What fear restrains you? Can you hesitate?
Your interest alone inspires my boldness.
    [*The impatient lover*]
While I am all aflame, whence comes your coldness?
    [*Incredulously*]
Are you afraid to trace my steps in exile?
    ARICIA: [*Reassuringly*]
Alas! How dear to me, my lord, were such
an exile! With what joyous transports I
should tie me to your fate; forgotten by
the world how glad I'd live! But—you and I—
    [*Hesitant*]
are not united in those lovely bonds—.
How can I then with honor fly with you?
    [*With pride*]
I know that I could free myself from out
your father's hands without a wound to strictest
idea of honor. It were not at all
to tear myself from breast of parents. Flight
is well allowed to those who fly a tyrant.
You love me, lord—my honor then must fear—
    HIPPOLYTUS: [*Interrupting as he understands*]
No, no, your reputation is too much
my care! A nobler hope has brought me here.

[*Running to her*]

Escape your foes, come with your husband. Free
of all our miseries, since Heaven wills,
we owe our plighted troth to no one else.

   [*With joy*]

Sure, wedding-rites are not attended always
by pomp of torches. At the gates of Troezen
amid the tombs where princes of my line
of old are sepulchred, a sacred temple
unknown to perjurers still stands; for there
no mortal dares to take an oath in vain.
The culpable wins sudden punishment,
and fears to find sure death there; treachery
knows nowhere curb more powerful. And there,

   [*Extending his hand to her, and drawing her to him*]

if you have faith in me, we'll go to seal
our solemn oath of our eternal love.
We'll take as witness the God who's worshipped there,
and pray that he be father to us both.
I'll call upon the name of Gods most sacred,
both chaste Diana and augustest Juno—
and all the Gods, who are the witnesses
of my affection, shall be called to stand
as guarantors of my most sacred vows.

   ARICIA: [*Who has been looking up at him, starts, and
looks offstage*]

The King is coming. Fly, prince, leave at once.
To hide my going I'll remain a moment.
Go now. But leave behind some faithful guide
to lead my untaught steps to where you'll be.

[*He kisses her hand. Exit* HIPPOLYTUS *quickly. Enter*
THESEUS]

THESEUS: Gods, lighten now my troubles, vouchsafe to
my eyes to see the truth I come to find!

ARICIA: [*Aside to* ISMENE]
Prepare all things, Ismene, for our flight.

[*Exit* ISMENE]

THESEUS: [*Advancing to her*]
Your color changes, and you seem abashed.
What was Hippolytus transacting here?

ARICIA: My lord, he took eternal leave of me.

THESEUS: [*Sarcastically*]
Your eyes could tame his rebel heart? *You* managed
to contrive he breathe what sighs he breathes for you?

ARICIA: [*Matching his sarcasm*]
My lord, I can't deny the truth; he's not
inherited *your* unjust hatred; he
has never treated me as though I were
a criminal.

THESEUS: Just so. And he has sworn
eternal love to you!

[*Changing his tone, he walks away from her*]
Don't count upon
a heart inconstant such as his. He's sworn
to others just as much as he has sworn
to you.

ARICIA: [*Plainly, in disbelief*]
He has, my lord?

THESEUS: You should have checked
his fickleness. How could you suffer so

dishonorable a sharing of your love?

ARICIA: [*Angrily following him*]
How could *you* suffer so dishonorable
a slander blacken life so pure as his?
Are you so ignorant of his good heart?
Can't you distinguish innocence like his
from crime? Must you alone be blinded by
an odious cloud that hides a virtue all
but you see radiant? It is too much
that you abandon him to wicked tongues!
Oh stop! Repent your homicidal prayers,
and fear, my lord,

   [*Pointing at him a warning finger*]

               yes, fear lest austere Heaven
hold hate enough to you to grant your prayers!
In anger often Heaven takes our victims—

   [*Threateningly*]

its gifts sometimes are punishment for sin.

THESEUS: In vain you seek to cover his attempt
at crime. Love blinds you in the ingrate's favor.
My certainty is based on evidence
beyond denying, palpable. I've seen—
I've seen tears fall which speak sincerest truth.

ARICIA: [*Renewing the threat*]
Take care, my lord. Your arm's invincible—
it's freed humanity of countless monsters.
But all are not destroyed; you've left alive
one who—.

   [*She stops on the verge of saying too much,
and walks away*]

Your son, my lord, forbids that I
continue. Well I know the reverence
he holds for you and I should too much blight
his heart if I dared finish what I say.
I copy his restraint, and flee your presence,
lest I feel constrained to break my silence.
    [*Exit*]

THESEUS: What did she mean? What veiled her speech,
                                    held checked
as often as begun? Would they confuse
my judgment by some vain pretense? Do they
connive to put me on the torture-rack?
But I, myself, despite my rigor—ah,
what plaintive voice cries from my depth of heart?
A secret pity both disturbs and stuns me.
Yes, I must question once again Oenone.
I wish for greater light upon this crime.
    [*Calling off*]
Guards, have Oenone come, and come alone.
    [*Enter* PANOPE]

PANOPE: [*Pausing at the couch. She speaks
in a stricken voice*]
I cannot tell what thing the Queen is planning.
I fear the worst from such a state as hers.
Most dire despair's depicted on her face;
death's pallor's on her cheeks. Just now Oenone,
disgraced, was driven from her sight, and threw
herself into the ocean's depths. Alas!
    [THESEUS *starts*]
We know not whence her impulse rash! The waves

forever now will hide her from our eyes.

THESEUS: [*Excited*]
What news is this?

PANOPE: Her death has no way calmed
the trouble in the Queen's disordered soul,
whose bitterness augments. Sometimes to soothe
her secret sorrow she embraces, while
she bathes with tears, her children. Suddenly,
abandoning her mother-love, she thrusts
them from her with a look of horror. Then
she walks about distracted, to and fro;
bewildered, her glance would seem to know none of us.
Three times she's written, thrice she's changed her mind
and torn the letter she'd begun. My lord,
I beg you see her! Come and save your queen!
    [*Exit*]

THESEUS: [*Impetuously*]
Just Gods! Oenone's dead and Phaedra longs
to die! If but my son could be *recalled*.
If he would but return to his defense!
If he would but come back to speak to me!
I'm ready now to hear him. Neptune, haste
not granting of your dreadful boon! I should
now plead you no more hearkened to my prayers.
Perhaps too easily I have believed
in evidence too little to be trusted.
Perhaps I've been too swift to raise my hands
in cruelty against you. Ah, with what
despair may not my prayers yet be followed?
    [*Enter* THERAMENES]

Act 5
scene 6

You, Theramenes! Where's my son?

[THERAMENES, *head bowed, does not answer*]

                                        To you
I have entrusted him since tenderest years.
But whence should flow these tears I see you weep?
Where is Hippolytus?

THERAMENES: [*Dully*]

                              Your care of him
is late and needless now—your words of love
are vain. Hippolytus is dead.

THESEUS: [*With a loud groan*]

                              Great Heavens!

THERAMENES: Alas! I've seen the best, most innocent
of men cut down before my very eyes . . .

THESEUS: My son is dead? When I was opening
to him my arms again, have angry Gods
made haste to end his life? What sudden blow,
what savage stroke has robbed me of my son?

THERAMENES: We'd scarcely passed through Troezen's
                                        gates—he in
his chariot, his sorrowed guards about him,
who emulated with their own his silence.
He followed the Mycenean road with thoughts
abstracted, leaving loose the reins upon
his horses' backs. These noble coursers who
one time obeyed with noble eagerness
his voice, were sad-eyed now, their heads abased,
and seemed to sympathize with his sad thoughts.
Then suddenly a dreadful cry came out
the depths of waves, shattering the stillness. Then

as from the very bosom of the earth,
to that dire cry a terrifying voice
replied in groans. Our blood froze in our hearts.
Our coursers hearing, bristled manes. And then
upon the ocean plain a mountain wave
churned up and rolled upon the shore, and broke,
and vomited midst spume a monster wild—
    [*Reliving the terror of the scene*]
its weighty brow was armed with threatening horns—
its body plated all with yellow scales—
a tameless bull and dragon violent—
its rump a mass of twisted winding coils—
prolonged its bellowing until the shore
began to shake. The sky beheld with horror
this savage beast, the earth with ferment, even
the air was venomed; terrified, the wave
which brought it, swift retreated. Everyone
took flight; without pretending futile courage,
each man sought refuge in a nearby temple—
except Hippolytus, who proved him worthy
of being son to a heroic father.
He stopped his chargers, seized his javelin,
and met the monster with a stroke hurled by
an arm of surest aim, and wounded it
deep in its side. With pain and rage the beast
sprang bellowing, and fell at once before
the horses' hooves, rolled over and revealed
his fiery throat, which spewed them over with flame
and blood and smoke. Fear maddened them, and deaf
for once to their loved master's voice, they knew

no more the bit. In vain attempts to rule them,
he spent himself. With bloody froth they stained
the curb. Some said they truly saw a God
who pricked their dusty flanks with goads in this
horrific chaos. Fear precipitated
the steeds across the rocks. The axle groaned
and broke. Undaunted still, Hippolytus
saw fly in splinters all his shattered car.
Entangled in the reins, he fell himself—

[*He sobs and pauses to contain himself*]

forgive my grief! That cruel picture shall
be everlastingly a source of tears
for me. I saw your luckless son, my lord—
I saw him dragged along by horses he
had fed with his own hand. He tried to call
them back; his voice but frightened them. They ran.
His body soon was all a mass of wounds.
The shore re-echoed our unhappy cries.
At last their headlong fury slackened. Then
they stopped, not distant from those ancient tombs
where lie his royal ancestors' remains
in frigid death. I ran there panting, his guard
behind me, led to him by tracing the track
of his most noble blood; the rocks were dyed
with it. The brambles, dripping gore, were hung
with his torn locks, their bloody spoils of triumph!
I reached him, called to him. He raised his hand
to me, he opened first his dying eyes,
then closed them suddenly. "The Gods," he said,
"have robbed me of my spotless life. Take care

when I am dead of poor Aricia.
Dear friend, the day my father knows he was
abused and weeps the wretched end of me,
his loyal son, accused by treachery,
tell him that to appease my blood, to calm
my plaintive shade, he must deal tenderly
with her, his prisoner. Tell him to give—."
And with that word the hero breathed his last;
and left within my arms—a sorry sight—
only a mangled body, the ruined spoils
of Heaven's wrath, which his own father scarce
would recognize to see before his eyes.

    THESEUS: My son! Dear hope of which
                        I've robbed myself!
Inexorable Gods who've served me well!
    [*With bitter grief*]
What wild remorse is yet reserved my days!

    THERAMENES: Then timidly Aricia came, my lord,
in flying from your wrath, to take before
the Gods him as her husband. As she neared
she saw the bloody grass all reeking—saw
(what sight for lover's eyes!) Hippolytus
extended pale, disfigured there. She tried
at first to doubt her eyes, nor knew the hero
adored by her; she saw Hippolytus,
yet still demanded where he was. Too sure
at last of what she saw before her, she
reproached the heavens with her woeful looks,
and chilled, and with a groan she fell in swoon
near death herself, right at her lover's feet.

Ismene, by her side and all in tears,
recalled her back to life—and back to sorrow.

[*Enter two* GUARDS;[40] *with great solemnity they take their
places on either side of the columns*]
And I, I came, in hate of life, to tell
his latest wish as I was charged, my lord,
when he lay dying, and acquit myself
of that unhappy task—.

[*During this speech,* THESEUS *walks brokenly to the
columns. The* GUARDS *pull back the curtains and reveal
the covered corpse of* HIPPOLYTUS]

                          But I perceive
his mortal enemy is coming here.

[*Looking offstage*]   *Act V Scene 7*

[*Enter* PHAEDRA, *followed by* PANOPE. THESEUS *staggers
away from the columns as he speaks.* PHAEDRA *leans
on couch*]

THESEUS: Well then, you triumph, and my son is dead!

---

[40] *This is the one place where I feel I have taken considerable
liberty with the play. In the original, Hippolytus' body is not
brought in. Theseus' remarks addressed to and about his son are
made rhetorically. On the English-speaking stage such rhetorical
drama would infallibly lame the end to this great tragedy. Taking
my cue from Theseus' line to Phaedra,* Mais, Madame, il est
mort, prenez votre victime (*But he is dead, madame: take your
victim*), *I have had Hippolytus' corpse revealed in the manner
indicated. The audiences in New York, however contrary this
may have been to the taste of Louis XIV's time, clearly approved.
It made for a very powerful, dramatic (rather than rhetorical)
conclusion; and, after all, did no violence to anything in the
play. A purist, however, may prefer to omit it. In point of fact,
all I have added is some stage directions!—B.D.N.G.*

What room have I for fear! What cruel doubt
alarms me now my heart exonerates him!
My lady, he is dead.

[*He turns back and rips off the covering of the corpse*]
                    Then take your victim!
Rejoice that he is lost, if justly doomed
or falsely. I'll permit my eyes be ever
deceived. I'll think him guilty since you have
accused him. I have cause enough to weep
that he is dead without my seeking light
which could not give him back to me who grieve him,
but hatefully might well augment my woe.
Let me, far from this shore and far from you,
flee from the image of my mangled son.
Confounded,

[*His hand over his eyes*]
                    persecuted by an anguished
memory, I wish to banish me
from all the world. All things rise up against
my cruelty to him. The glory of
my name itself will only aggravate
my punishment. Were I less known to men,
I'd have some hope to hide myself. I hate
the very care with which the Gods saw fit
to honor me. I go to weep their favor
so murderous to me, and weary them
no more with futile prayers. Whatever they
might do for me, their dreadful kindness could
not pay me back for all they've robbed me of.

PHAEDRA: No, Theseus—I must break my unjust silence.

Your son shall own again his innocence.
He never yet was guilty.

THESEUS: [*Without looking at her*]
                              Wretched father!
And on your word I judged him! Cruel woman!
Think you that your excuse—

PHAEDRA: [*During this speech, she staggers, her words coming more and more painfully*]
                              My minutes, Theseus,
are numbered. It was I who cast an eye
corrupt, incestuous, upon your chaste
and blameless son. The Heavens burned within
my breast that fatal passion; vile Oenone
contrived the rest. She feared Hippolytus,
my madness known to him, might swift reveal
a love which caused him only horror. She
perfidiously took advantage of
my weakness and made haste to bring the charge
against him to your ears. She's punished now,
though all too lightly for her crime; she fled
my wrath and found escape in suicide.
The sword should long ago have cut me down,
but I allowed suspected virtue groan.
I wished to walk a slower way to death
so I might still make plain my deep remorse.
[*A spasm of pain*]
I've taken—I have made to race within
my burning veins a poison which Medea[41]
brought into Athens. Now already has

---

[41] *wife of Jason. She had mastered the science of potions.*

the venom reached my heart, an icy chill
spreads over my dying heart; already I
can see but through a mist the Heavens and
the husband whom my presence outrages.
And death, which veils the light of day before
my eyes,

   [*She staggers toward him with outstretched hands, as
though blind*]

               and renders back again to day
the purity my eyes have foully sullied—

   [*She collapses before his feet. She dies*]

   PANOPE: She's dying, lord.

   THESEUS: [*Too horrified to look at her body*]

                         If only with her death
might die the memory of her black deeds!
Too well I know the truth at last. Let's go
to mingle tears with my unhappy son's
wronged blood. Let's go embrace his dear remains,
and expiate my folly. Tender him
those honors he has merited! To appease
his angry shade, despite the unjust plots
which were her family's, Aricia
shall be to me a daughter from this day.

                    [CURTAIN]

"The performances of the Comédie Francaise
traditionally end with this line, the rest being
regarded as anticlimactic" Mack, et al
World Masterpieces 2. p. 1304